Moon Cycle Cookbook

Align Your Kitchen with Lunar Cycles for Nourishing Cuisine and Spiritual Wellbeing

By: Angela R. Millen

TABLE OF CONTENTS

Table Of Contents 2

Introduction 5

Moon Cycle Cookbook: Recipes 6

   1. Lunar Lemon Sorbet 7

   2. Dark Sky Black Bean Soup 9

   3. Celestial Chia Seed Pudding 11

   4. Cosmic Cauliflower Bites 13

   5. Night Sky Blueberry Smoothie 15

   6. Twilight Tempeh Tacos 17

   7. Lunar Eclipse Dark Chocolate Mousse 19

   8. Midnight Mint Matcha Latte 21

   9. Starry Night Sushi Rolls 23

   10. Moonbeam Mushroom Risotto 25

   11. Crescent-shaped Croissant Sandwiches 27

   12. Luminescent Lentil Curry 29

   15. Illuminated Mango Salsa 35

   16. Crescent Cauliflower Crust Pizza 36

   17. Glowing Ginger Carrot Soup 38

   18. Radiating Raspberry Oat Bars 40

   19. Lemon-Garlic Shrimp Skewers 42

   20. Crescent Cucumber Canapés 43

   21. Quarter Moon Quesadillas 44

   22. Stellar Sesame Noodle Salad 46

   23. Luminary Lemon Chicken 48

   24. Radiant Roasted Veggies 50

   25. Lunar Lentil Loaf 52

   26. Quarter Phase Quinoa Pilaf 54

   27. Sparkling Strawberry Salad 56

   28. Lunar Eclipse Empanadas 58

   29. Sizzlin' Steak Stir-Fry 60

30. Brilliant Barley Bowl 62
31. Luminous Lemon Bars 64
32. Homemade Granola Bars 66
33. Radiant Ramen Bowl 68
34. Gibbous Moon Garlic Bread 70
35. Enchanted Eggplant Parmesan 71
36. Brilliant Banana Bread 72
37. Lunar Lavender Latte 74
38. Glowing Green Goddess Salad 75
39. Luminescent Lemon Pepper Chicken 77
40. Illuminated Iceberg Lettuce Wraps 79
41. Full Moon Fruit Tart 81
42. Moonlit Miso Soup 83
43. Brightest Buddha Bowl 85
44. Lunar Eclipse Lava Cake 87
45. Illuminating Ice Cream Sandwiches 89
46. Full Moon Fettuccine Alfredo 91
47. Celestial Charcuterie Board 92
48. Radiant Ramen Noodles 94
49. Lunar Lasagna Roll-Ups 96
50. Midnight Moon Pies 98
51. Waning Walnut Waffles 100
52. Glow-out Granola Parfait 102
53. Subsiding Spinach Salad 104
54. Lunar Lemon Poppy Seed Muffins 106
55. Diminishing Dark Chocolate Truffles 108
56. Fading Fig Flatbread 110
57. Crescent Carrot Cake 112
58. Dwindling Dahl Soup 114
59. Vanishing Veggie Stir-Fry 116
60. Waning Walnut Brownies 118
61. Last Quarter Quiche 120

62. Lunar Lox Bagel Sandwiches 122
63. Fading Fruit Smoothie Bowl 123
64. Dimming Dill Dip 125
65. Quarter Phase Quinoa Salad 126
66. Receding Radish Wraps 128
67. Lunar Lavender Lemonade 130
68. Disappearing Date Bars 131
69. DIMINISHED DARK CHERRY CRISP 133
70. Wilted Waning Watercress Soup 135
The End 137

INTRODUCTION

Moon Cycle Cookbook is a tribute to the moon cycle and how it relates to our identities—physical, mental, and spiritual—through food. This cookbook is a guide to eating seasonally and healthily while respecting the cycles of the natural world, not just a compilation of recipes. People have respected the moon for its magical attributes and the ways it has influenced their worldview throughout history and space. The moon has always held a unique position in human awareness, from prehistoric rituals to contemporary scientific studies. The cycle of the moon, which lasts for around 29.5 days from one new moon to the next, is one of the most obvious ways we could feel its influence.

Every phase of the moon has a distinct energy and meaning, ranging from new to waxing crescent, first quarter, full moon, waning gibbous, decreasing crescent, and lastly, waning gibbous. We'll look at how eating in accordance with the moon cycle may improve our health and strengthen our bonds with the natural world in this cuisine.

Having stated that, what triggers the moon's phase changes? By realizing the close relationship that exists between our bodies and the natural world, we can discover the solution. Our energy levels, emotions, and circadian rhythms all change with the moon's rising and setting. We may connect with this innate rhythm and enhance our lives' harmony, vigor, and balance by incorporating lunar rhythms into the way we cook and eat.

A cookbook called "Moon Cycle Cookbook" is an assortment of dishes created to coincide with the moon's phases. Each recipe has been carefully chosen to respect the moon cycle. While robust and anchored feasts are ideal for the full moon, which symbolizes plenty and completeness, light and refreshing meals are ideal for the new moon, which represents new beginnings and fresh begins.

No matter how experienced you are in the kitchen, there is something acceptable for you to try on these pages. Along with instructions for bringing awareness and intention into your cooking, each dish offers advice on how to tap into the special energy of the matching moon phase.

Join us on this culinary adventure that draws inspiration from the moon's phases. Let us nourish our bodies, brains, and spirits in accordance with the cosmic cycles and honor the moon's power.

MOON CYCLE COOKBOOK : RECIPES

NEW MOON RECIPES:

1. LUNAR LEMON SORBET

INGREDIENTS:

- 1 cup freshly squeezed lemon juice
- Zest of 2 lemons
- 1 cup granulated sugar
- 2 cups water
- Fresh mint leaves

INSTRUCTIONS:

1. The simple syrup is made by heating water and sugar in a medium pot to a boil.
2. To make a simple syrup, periodically swirl the sugar once it has completely dissolved.
3. Once the sugar has dissolved fully, remove the saucepan from the heat source and let the simple syrup cool to room temperature.
4. Transfer the zest and juice of the freshly squeezed lemons into a mixing bowl.

Mix the Ingredients:

1. Transfer the chilled simple syrup into the lemon zest and juice bowl. Toss to blend thoroughly.
2. The mixture should be chilled.
3. Cover the bowl and refrigerate for at least one hour to ensure it's cool enough before churning.

Making Sorbet Churn:

1. Transfer the cold mixture into your ice cream machine and follow the manufacturer's instructions. The mixture typically needs 20 to 30 minutes to reach sorbet consistency.

Freeze:

2. After churning, pour the sorbet into a container that can be frozen.
3. Place a lid or piece of plastic wrap immediately over the container to avoid ice crystals accumulating on the sorbet's surface.
4. Allow the sorbet to solidify in the freezer for three to four hours.

Serving:

1. Take the sorbet out of the freezer a few minutes before serving to soften and make scooping easier.
2. Spoon the Lunar Lemon Sorbet into glasses or bowls; if preferred, garnish with fresh mint leaves and serve right away.

NOTE:

- The sorbet keeps well in the freezer for up to a week. However, it's best consumed within a few days of preparation for the most incredible texture and flavour.
- Savour this delightfully zesty Lunar Lemon Sorbet whenever you're craving something refreshing during the New Moon period!

2. DARK SKY BLACK BEAN SOUP

INGREDIENTS:

- 2 cans black beans, drained and rinsed
- 1 tablespoon olive oil
- 1 onion, diced
- 3 cloves garlic, minced
- 1 red bell pepper, diced
- 1 carrot, diced
- 1 teaspoon ground cumin
- 1 teaspoon smoked paprika
- 1/2 teaspoon chilli powder
- 4 cups vegetable or chicken broth
- 1 can diced tomatoes
- Salt and pepper to taste
- Fresh cilantro, chopped
- Sour cream or yoghurt
- Lime wedges

INSTRUCTIONS:

1. Get the beans ready.
2. Thoroughly drain and rinse the canned black beans. Put away.

Aromatics sautéed:

1. Olive oil should be heated in a big saucepan or Dutch oven over medium heat.
2. Add the carrot, chopped onion, red bell pepper, and garlic. After 5 to 7 minutes of sautéing
3. , the veggies should soften.
4. Combine chilli powder, smoked paprika, and ground cumin to season the vegetables. Cook until aromatic, one or two more minutes.
5. Add the chopped tomatoes, their juices, black beans, and vegetable or chicken broth to a saucepan and simmer. Toss to mix thoroughly.
6. As soon as the mixture reaches a boil, lower the heat. To let the flavors marry, cover and simmer for twenty to twenty-five minutes.
7. Mix (optional): You may use an immersion blender to briefly blend the soup in the saucepan for a smoother consistency. Alternatively, you may move some of the soup into a blender, puree it, and then put it back into the pot.
8. After tasting the soup, adjust the seasoning with salt and pepper before serving.

9. Spoon Dark Sky Black Bean Soup into individual bowls. As a garnish, feel free to add some finely chopped fresh cilantro and a dollop of sour cream or yoghurt.
10. To enable the soup to be poured over the lime wedges, they are presented sideways.

NOTE:

- This soup pairs beautifully with a slice of crusty bread or a side dish of tortilla chips. It's perfect to enjoy outside on a chilly night under the stars or at different moon phases. To fit your needs, taste the spices and adjust.

3. CELESTIAL CHIA SEED PUDDING

INGREDIENTS:

- 1/4 cup chia seeds
- 1 cup unsweetened almond milk
- 1 tablespoon maple syrup or honey
- 1/2 teaspoon vanilla extract
- Mixed fresh berries for topping
- Edible flowers or mint leaves

INSTRUCTIONS:

1. To make the Chia Seed Base, put the chia seeds, almond milk, honey, maple syrup, and vanilla essence in a jar or mixing bowl.
2. Stir the dish well to ensure the chia seeds and liquid are fully incorporated.
3. Refrigerate the jar or dish for at least two hours or overnight, covered. For the first fifteen minutes, stir occasionally to avoid clumping.
4. Put the Pudding Together: After the chia seeds have absorbed the liquid and thickened to the consistency of Pudding, give the mixture a thorough swirl.
5. You may adjust the Pudding's consistency by adding extra almond milk if it's too thick.
6. To serve, divide the Celestial Chia Seed Pudding across glasses or serving dishes.
7. Add a variety of fresh berries to each serving, arranging them in an attractive way over the Pudding.
8. Garnish (optional): Add some edible flowers or a few mint leaves to the Pudding for an additional touch of heavenly beauty.

Savor:

1. You may serve the Pudding immediately or put it in the fridge to serve it later.
2. This Pudding is an excellent treat to savour throughout different moon phases. It can be kept covered in the refrigerator for up to three days.

NOTE:

- Nuts, granola, shredded coconut, sliced fruits, and other toppings can create the versatile chia seed pudding. You may adjust the sweetness by adding more or less honey or maple syrup to suit your taste.
- An eye-catching meal for any moon phase celebration, the celestial touch comes from the beauty of the mixed fresh berries and optional edible flower garnish.

4. COSMIC CAULIFLOWER BITES

INGREDIENTS:

- 1 medium head cauliflower, cut into florets
- 1 cup breadcrumbs
- 1/2 cup grated Parmesan cheese
- 2 teaspoons paprika
- 1 teaspoon garlic powder
- 1/2 teaspoon onion powder
- Salt and pepper to taste
- 2 large eggs
- Cooking spray or olive oil

INSTRUCTIONS:

Warm up the oven:

1. Turn the oven down to 200°C or 400°F. Use cooking spray to lightly oil or line a baking sheet with parchment paper.
2. Prepare the cauliflower blossoms.
3. To ensure consistent cooking, chop the cauliflower into bite-sized florets, paying attention to their relative uniformity in size.
4. Get the coating mixture ready.
5. In a small basin, combine breadcrumbs, nutritional yeast or grated Parmesan cheese, paprika, onion and garlic powders, salt, and pepper.

Apply a coat to the cauliflower:

1. Beat the eggs in another dish. You can also make flax eggs by combining 2 teaspoons of ground flaxseed meal with 6 tablespoons of water and letting it sit for a while to thicken.
2. After dipping each cauliflower floret into the beaten eggs (or flax egg mixture), let any extra egg drop off.
3. To coat the cauliflower florets uniformly, roll them in the breadcrumb mixture and gently press them to bind.

Cook the Cosmic Bites of Cauliflower:

1. Leaving room between each piece, arrange the coated cauliflower florets in a single layer on the preheated baking sheet.
2. To make the cauliflower bits crispier, either mist the tops with cooking spray or lightly drizzle them with olive oil.

Cook in the Oven:

1. Preheat the oven and bake the cauliflower for 20 to 25 minutes, or until it's soft and the coating is crispy and golden.
2. Take the Cosmic Cauliflower Bites out of the oven and let them cool a little before serving.
3. Present them as a delightful snack or starter under a starry night sky during different moon phases.

NOTE:

- ➢ You may pair these versatile Cosmic Cauliflower Bites with your favourite dipping sauce, spicy aioli, ranch, or marinara. Enjoy their crunchy, salty taste during your wonderful get-togethers! Taste and adjust spices and flavours accordingly.

5. NIGHT SKY BLUEBERRY SMOOTHIE

INGREDIENTS:

- 1 cup frozen blueberries
- 1 ripe banana, peeled and sliced
- 1/2 cup plain Greek yogurt
- 1/2 cup almond milk
- 1 tablespoon honey or maple syrup
- 1/2 teaspoon vanilla extract
- 1 tablespoon chia seeds
- Edible glitter or edible pearl dust

INSTRUCTIONS:

1. Prepare the ingredients: Before creating the smoothie, slice your banana and put it in the freezer for around an hour if it isn't frozen.
2. Combine the ingredients: Frozen blueberries, almond milk, chia seeds, peanut butter, banana slices, Greek yoghurt, vanilla extract, and honey or maple syrup (if preferred) should all be combined together and blended.
3. Process quickly until the mixture is smooth and creamy. If the consistency is too thick, add a tiny quantity of almond milk to get the desired thickness.

How to Produce the Night Sky Effect:

1. Blend in a small amount of edible glitter or pearl dust for an eye-catching "night sky" appearance. To make the smoothie look like a starry night, pulse the blender long enough to mix in the glitter.

Provide:

- The Night Sky Blueberry Smoothie should be poured into glasses.
- Feel free to top it with extra edible glitter or pearl dust for a special touch.

Enjoy yourself:

1. Take a sip of this smoothie with a cosmic theme and imagine how beautiful the night sky looks at different times of the moon.

NOTE:

- This smoothie looks gorgeous, but it's packed with antioxidants from the blueberries and minerals from the chia seeds. To suit your taste, you may change the sweetness by modifying the amount of honey or maple syrup. To make it your own cosmic masterpiece, feel free to add extra fruits or nutrients!

6. TWILIGHT TEMPEH TACOS

INGREDIENTS:

For the Tempeh Filling:

- 8 ounces tempeh, crumbled
- 2 tablespoons olive oil
- 2 cloves garlic, minced
- 1 small onion, finely chopped
- 1 teaspoon ground cumin
- 1 teaspoon chilli powder
- 1/2 teaspoon paprika
- 1/2 teaspoon dried oregano
- Salt and pepper to taste
- 1/4 cups tomato sauce or crushed tomatoes
- 2 tbsp. water

For Serving:

- 8 small corn or flour tortillas
- Shredded lettuce
- Diced tomatoes
- Sliced avocado
- Chopped cilantro
- Lime wedges
- Salsa or hot sauce (optional)

INSTRUCTIONS:

Tempeh Filling Preparation:

1. In a pan over medium heat and preheat the olive oil. Add the minced garlic and stir once the garlic and onion begin to soften in the pan.
2.
3. Fry the crumbled tempeh in a pan over medium heat, tossing occasionally, until it begins to brown, about 5 minutes.
4.

For the Filling:

1. Season the tempeh with salt, pepper, chilli powder, paprika, dried oregano, and powdered cumin. Stir the spices thoroughly to distribute them evenly.
2. Before adding water, stir in the tomato sauce (or chopped tomatoes). Mix everything well to combine the flavours. Stir and cook for another two or three minutes until everything is boiled and mixed.
3. Warm the tortillas in the oven or griddle per the package directions while the tempeh filling cooks.

Grill or Saute the Meat:

1. Spoon some tempeh filling with seasonings onto each tortilla that has been warmed.
2. Arrange the sliced avocado, chopped cilantro, diced tomatoes, lime juice, freshly squeezed over the top of the tacos and shredded lettuce.

Place the order:

1. Garnish the Twilight Tempeh Tacos with more salsa or spicy sauce, if preferred.
2. Note that these Twilight Tempeh Tacos may be personalized according to your taste by adding any toppings or garnishes you like. A protein-rich and tasty alternative to traditional taco fillings, tempeh is perfect for taco nights under the moon or any other moonlight celebration. Adjust the seasonings to your liking to savour these tasty vegetarian tacos.

7. LUNAR ECLIPSE DARK CHOCOLATE MOUSSE

INGREDIENTS:

- 7 ounces (200g) good quality dark chocolate, chopped
- 1/4 cup (60ml) water
- 3 large eggs separated
- 2 tablespoons granulated sugar (adjust to taste)
- 1 teaspoon pure vanilla extract
- A pinch of salt
- Optional garnish: whipping cream or whipped coconut cream.
- Fresh berries for garnish (optional)
- Edible silver or gold dust for a celestial touch (optional)

INSTRUCTIONS:

1. Pour the water and chopped dark chocolate into a heatproof dish. To melt the chocolate, place the bowl over a saucepan of boiling water or use a double boiler. Stir from time to time to guarantee a smooth consistency. Remove the bowl from the burner and let it to cool.
2. Beat the Eggs: Beat the yolks and whites of the eggs separately on separate plates while the chocolate cools.
3. Beat chocolate and egg yolks together.
4. Once the chocolate has somewhat cooled, use a fork to completely combine each egg yolk. Add the vanilla essence and stir.
5. Beat the egg whites with a clean, dry whisk or an electric mixer set to medium-high speed until soft peaks begin to form. Once firm peaks start to form, stir in a little amount of salt.
6. Addition of Sugar: Continue whipping the egg whites and gradually whisk in the powdered sugar. Until the tips shine, put in a lot of work.
7. Gently incorporate 1/3 of the whisked egg whites into the chocolate blend.
8. When folding in the remaining beaten egg whites, take care not to deflate the mixture.
9. Chill the Dark Chocolate Mousse for Lunar Eclipse in the fridge before serving. Transfer to individual bowls or glasses.
10. The mousse has to set for at least two or three hours in the refrigerator.
11. You may add an ethereal touch to the mousse by decorating it with fresh berries, whipped cream or coconut cream, and edible silver or gold dust before serving.
12. Try this velvety Lunar Eclipse Dark Chocolate Mousse for a decadent dessert appropriate for a starry occasion or any celebration.

NOTE:
- ➢ If you adore chocolate, you will savour this rich and luscious mousse. This dessert is ideal for hosting guests or indulging in a celestial-themed treat during a lunar eclipse because it is best enjoyed cold and can be made ahead of time. Just add more or less sugar to make it sweeter or less sweet.

8. MIDNIGHT MINT MATCHA LATTE

INGREDIENTS:

- 1 teaspoon matcha green tea powder
- 1 tablespoon hot water
- 1 cup milk
- 1/4 teaspoon pure peppermint extract
- 1 tablespoon honey, maple syrup, or sweetener of choice
- Whipped cream
- Fresh mint leaves for garnish
- Dark chocolate shavings

INSTRUCTIONS:

1. Get the Matcha Paste Ready: Strain the matcha green tea powder into a cup or basin to eliminate lumps.
2. Bring the water to a simmer before adding the matcha powder. Whip the matcha with a spoon or a bamboo whisk until it forms a ball for a silky paste free of clumps.
3. Bring the milk to a simmer in a small pot over medium heat without boiling it. You can also put the milk in a container that is safe to be placed in the microwave and give it a quick blast.
4. Mix the matcha paste and pour it into the mug while the milk is heating.
5. Sweeten matcha milk with peppermint extract, honey, maple syrup, or any other sweetener. Combine all of the ingredients by stirring vigorously.

Optional:

1. Wash the mint matcha latte with a milk frother for a creamier texture.
2. Fill a serving cup with the Midnight Mint Matcha Latte and serve.
3. An optional garnish is a dab of whipped cream on the latte to make it richer.
4. To make it very special, garnish it with fresh mint leaves or dark chocolate shavings.

NOTE:

- Experience the tranquillity of midnight with a sip of our Midnight Mint Matcha Latte, a blend of relaxed and calming tastes that will transport you to a moonlight sky or a peaceful moment.
- Keep in mind that you may customize the amount of sweetness and mintiness to your liking. You may also try out other milk (almond, oat, coconut, etc) to see what works best for you. A

delightful late-night heavenly treat, this drink also contains the antioxidants found in matcha green tea and has a relaxing effect.

9. STARRY NIGHT SUSHI ROLLS

INGREDIENTS:

- ❖ Sushi rice
- ❖ Nori (seaweed) sheets
- ❖ Sushi-grade fish (e.g., tuna, salmon), thinly sliced or your choice of fillings (e.g., cucumber, avocado, crab sticks)
- ❖ Rice vinegar
- ❖ Sugar
- ❖ Salt
- ❖ Sesame seeds (black and white)
- ❖ Edible gold or silver flakes (optional for decoration)
- ❖ Bamboo sushi rolling mat

INSTRUCTIONS:

1. Follow the package directions to cook the sushi rice. After the rice is boiled, add a combination of sugar, salt, and vinegar according to your taste. Set aside the rice to cool.
2. Get the Fillings Ready:
3. Prepare fillings like cucumber, avocado, and crab sticks, or slice sushi-grade fish into thin strips.
4. Before assembling your sushi rolls, find a clean surface or a bamboo sushi rolling mat. Then, lay a sheet of nori, shiny side down.
5. After you put down the nori sheet, evenly distribute the seasoned sushi rice, being sure to leave a little border at the top edge.
6. Fillings: Spread the fillings you've selected on the bottom two-thirds of the nori sheet coated with rice.
7. Start at the bottom border of the bamboo mat and roll away from yourself as you firmly roll the nori and ingredients to make sushi. Gently press down on the roll to form it.
8. Separate the Rolls: Using a sharp, moist knife, Cut each sushi roll into individual pieces, approximately 1 inch thick.
9. Make Stunning Starry Night Scenes:
10. Top the sliced sushi rolls with a mixture of black and white sesame seeds for a starry night sky effect.
11. As an optional garnish, you can make the sushi rolls seem more elegant by lightly dusting them with edible gold or silver flakes, creating a glittering appearance that resembles stars or the universe.
12. Place the sushi rolls in a starry night pattern on a dish to serve.

NOTE:
- ➢ Consider that the idea of a starry night might be reflected in any imaginative fills and presentation. You can make a stunning night sky image using black and white sesame seeds on top of rice. Enjoy this visually stunning sushi roll presentation at a party with a space theme or while stargazing at night. Use different ingredients and fillings to find what you like most.

10. MOONBEAM MUSHROOM RISOTTO

INGREDIENTS:

- 1 ½ cups Arborio rice
- 4 cups vegetable or chicken broth
- 2 tablespoons unsalted butter
- 2 tablespoons olive oil
- 1 onion, finely chopped
- 2 cloves garlic, minced
- 8 ounces assorted mushrooms (cremini, shiitake, etc.), sliced
- 1/2 cup dry white wine (optional)
- 1/2 cup grated Parmesan cheese
- 2 tablespoons fresh parsley, chopped
- Salt and pepper to taste
- Truffle oil for drizzling (optional for added flavour)

INSTRUCTIONS:

Get the Broth Ready:

1. Put the chicken or vegetable broth in a saucepan and cook it over low heat until it's hot.
2. To sauté the mushrooms, combine the olive oil and butter in a big saucepan and cook over medium heat for 1 tablespoon.
3. Coat the onion and garlic with the minced parts. The onions should be sautéed until they become slightly transparent.
4. Put Mushrooms in the Pan: When the sliced mushrooms are ready, toss them into the pan and cook until they brown and become soft, draining any excess liquid.
5. Toast the Arborio rice by tossing it with the mushrooms in a pan. Once the rice grains turn translucent around the edges, stir and cook for another two or three minutes.
6. Optional: Deglaze with White Wine: Pour the white wine into the skillet, rice, and mushrooms. Keep stirring until the rice soaks up all of the wine.
7. Risotto is made by slowly adding heated broth to a pan, ladleful at a time while constantly swirling so the rice soaks up the liquid.
8. The rice should be creamy and cooked to an al dente texture, so keep adding stock and tossing for around 18-20 minutes.

Pile on the Risotto:

1. Combine the grated Parmesan cheese (or nutritional yeast for a vegan version) with the remaining tablespoon of butter and stir until well blended.
2. Season to taste with salt and pepper.
3. Reserve for sprinkling:
4. Top the Moonbeam Mushroom Risotto with some freshly chopped parsley.
5. Optional: sprinkle with some truffle oil before serving for an extra touch and increased taste.
6. Indulge immediately in the warm, creamy, earthy Moonbeam Mushroom Risotto to savour the aromas transporting you to a moonlight night.

NOTE:

➢ Moonbeam Mushroom Risotto, with its velvety Arborio rice and earthy mushrooms, is ideal for a starry night in or a dinner party themed around the night sky. Whether you make it more or less mushroom-y or add various kinds depends on your tastes. Adding truffle oil elevates the meal to a new level of decadence with its rich, complex taste.

WAXING CRESCENT RECIPES:

11. CRESCENT-SHAPED CROISSANT SANDWICHES

INGREDIENTS:

- 1 can (8 oz) refrigerated crescent rolls
- Sliced deli meats (ham, turkey, roast beef) or vegetarian alternatives
- Shredded cheese (cheddar, Swiss, provolone) or vegan cheese, if preferred
- Lettuce leaves
- Tomato slices
- Mayonnaise, mustard, or preferred condiments
- Optional additional fillings: avocado slices, cucumber, bacon, etc.

INSTRUCTIONS:

1. Get the Oven Ready: Follow the directions on the crescent roll packaging to get the oven ready.
2. Get the Crescent Rolls ready:
3. Once you have a clean surface, unroll the crescent dough. Use the perforated lines as guides to divide it into the pre-cut triangles.
4. To assemble the sandwiches, spread a little condiment (mustard, mayonnaise, etc.) into each triangle of crescent rolls.
5. Include Fillings:
6. Use one triangle to stack your preferred fillings—sliced deli meat, cheese, lettuce, tomato, etc.
7. Roll into a crescent shape by beginning at the broad end of each triangle and rolling up with the contents inside.
8. Place the crescent-shaped sandwiches on a parchment-lined or lightly greased baking sheet before baking.
9. Crescent rolls should be baked in a preheated oven according to the package directions, usually until golden brown.
10. Removing the crescent-shaped croissant sandwiches from the oven after baking allows them to cool for a few minutes before serving.

Take pleasure in:

- These simple and tasty croissant sandwiches are great for a fast lunch or snack and may be served hot or at room temperature.

Take note:

- To make the sandwiches exactly how you want them, use the meats, cheeses, and vegetables you choose. These croissant sandwiches, which are shaped like crescents, are perfect for lunch, breakfast, or any time you're in the mood for a portable, delicious meal.

12. LUMINESCENT LENTIL CURRY

INGREDIENTS:

- 1 cup dry lentils (green or red), rinsed and drained
- 2 tablespoons vegetable oil
- 1 onion, finely chopped
- 3 cloves garlic, minced
- 1 tablespoon fresh ginger, grated
- 2 tomatoes, chopped
- 1 can (14 oz) coconut milk
- 2 cups vegetable broth
- 2 teaspoons curry powder
- 1 teaspoon ground turmeric
- 1 teaspoon ground cumin
- 1 teaspoon ground coriander
- 1/2 teaspoon chilli powder (adjust to taste)
- Salt and pepper to taste
- Fresh cilantro leaves for garnish
- Cooked rice or naan bread for serving

INSTRUCTIONS:

1. Begin by rinsing the lentils thoroughly to prepare them.
2. In a large skillet or saucepan, sauté the aromatics in vegetable oil over medium heat. Add the chopped onion and sauté until it starts to turn transparent.
3. Whisk in the minced garlic and grated ginger and continue whisking for another minute or until fragrant.
4. Toss in the spices when the chopped tomatoes have softened in the pan.
5. Curry powder, ground cumin, turmeric, coriander, and chilli powder should be added. Mix thoroughly. Continue heating for an additional minute to toast the spices.
6. After rinsing, add the lentils, spices, and aromatics to the pot; stir to combine. The lentils should be tender, so do not cook them too long.
7. The vegetable stock and coconut milk should be combined. Raise the
8. heat to high, then reduce it to low and simmer.
9. Once the lentils are soft and the curry has thickened to your preference, cook, cover, and cook over low heat for 20-25 minutes. Once some time has passed, give Everything a good stir.
10. Before serving, taste the lentil curry and add salt and pepper as needed.
11. Warm up some rice or naan to go with your Light-Up Lentil Curry.

12. Chopped cilantro leaves are a nice garnish for each plate.

Take pleasure in:

Indulge in the soothing flavours of this Luminescent Lentil Curry, a vibrant and nourishing dish thanks to its abundance of spices and silky coconut milk.

NOTE:
- Please note that the spice levels can be adjusted to suit your taste. Vegetables like bell peppers, spinach, or carrots can be added to this curry to enhance its flavour and nutritional value. Whether you're in the mood for a filling lentil dish or just want something substantial to eat for supper, this recipe will do the trick.

13. CRESCENT MOON COOKIES

INGREDIENTS:

- 1 cup unsalted butter, softened
- 1/2 cup powdered sugar
- 2 teaspoons vanilla extract
- 2 cups all-purpose flour
- 1/4 teaspoon salt
- 1 cup finely chopped nuts
- Additional powdered sugar for coating

INSTRUCTIONS:

1. Bring the oven up to temperature: Get the oven up to 350°F (175°C).
2. Gather Ingredients:
3. Whip the powdered sugar, vanilla extract, and softened butter in a bowl until the mixture is light and airy.
4. Whisk the all-purpose flour and salt in a separate dish to mix the dry ingredients.
5. To make the dough, cream the sugar and butter together. Then, slowly add the flour mixture. Blend until a tacky dough is formed.
6. Toss in the Nuts: After mixing the cookie dough, gently fold in the finely chopped nuts.
7. To create the cookies, flatten a tiny amount of dough into a ball. Then, using gentle pressure and tapering the ends to produce points, shape it into a crescent moon shape.
8. Leave space between each cookie when you place the formed crescent cookies onto an ungreased baking sheet.
9. Place the crescent moon cookies in the oven and bake for 12–15 minutes, or until they are brown around the edges.
10. Let the cookies set on the baking pan for a few minutes before coating.
11. While still warm, carefully coat each cookie equally with more powdered sugar. After they have cooled entirely, set them on a wire rack.
12. Before serving, let the Crescent Moon Cookies cool and coat them.

Take pleasure in:

These buttery crescent-shaped cookies have a wonderful nutty flavour and are fantastic on their own or served as an accompaniment at parties with a heavenly theme.

NOTE:

Be advised that these Crescent Moon Cookies would perfectly complement any celebration with a space theme or other celestial theme. To make it more unique, you may use various nuts or add edible glitter or silver or gold dust for a magical touch. If sealed properly, these cookies will keep for a long time and are perfect for sharing as a snack or gift.

14. RADIANT RICE PAPER WRAPS

INGREDIENTS:

- Rice paper wrappers
- 1 cup rice vermicelli noodles, cooked according to package instructions
- Substitute 1 cup of cooked and shredded chicken or tofu for a vegetarian option.
- Assorted vegetables (such as bell peppers, carrots, cucumber, lettuce, avocado, etc.), thinly sliced or julienned
- Fresh herbs (mint, basil, cilantro), chopped
- Optional additions: sliced mango, shrimp, or any preferred fillings
- Soy sauce or hoisin sauce for dipping (optional)
- Peanut or almond dipping sauce (optional)

INSTRUCTIONS:

1. Before you start, get the rice paper:
2. Heat a small bowl or pie plate and fill it with water.
3. To make one rice paper wrapper malleable, dip it into warm water for ten to fifteen seconds. After removing it, set it on a moist, cleaned kitchen towel.
4. Gather the Ingredients for the Wraps: Spread a little cooked rice vermicelli noodle mixture on the bottom third of the pliable rice paper wrapper.
5. Top the noodles with shredded chicken or tofu.
6. Garnish with Vegetables and Herbs: Arrange a variety of thinly sliced vegetables and herbs across the tofu or chicken wrapper in a longitudinal pattern.
7. Optional Ingredients: Top the veggie layer with other ingredients, such as sliced mango or shrimp.
8. Begin at the bottom edge of the rice paper wrapper and roll it firmly over the contents, folding in the edges as you go.
9. This will produce a clean cylinder.
10. Proceed with the remaining rice paper wraps and contents in the same manner, and then serve.
11. Before serving, cut the Radiant Rice Paper Wraps in half lengthwise or keep them intact.
12. Place the wraps on a dish and, if desired, top with hoisin sauce, peanut butter, or soy sauce.

Take pleasure in:

Whether you're hosting a party with a space theme or just want something light to eat, these Radiant Rice Paper Wraps will surely be a hit.

NOTE:

1. Please feel free to add veggies, proteins, or other things you like to the fillings. These wraps are colourful and adaptable for a light and tasty meal. If you want more taste, you may change up the dipping sauces. They're perfect for preparing in advance and keeping in the fridge for up to an hour before you serve them.

15. ILLUMINATED MANGO SALSA

INGREDIENTS:

- 2 ripe mangoes, diced
- 1 red bell pepper, diced
- 1/2 red onion, finely chopped
- 1 jalapeño pepper, seeded and minced (adjust to taste)
- 1/4 cup fresh cilantro, chopped
- Juice of 2 limes
- If you'd like it sweeter, you may add a spoonful of honey or agave syrup.
- Salt and pepper to taste

INSTRUCTIONS:

2. Get Everything Ready: Slice the ripe mangoes into small pieces. Peel and chop the red bell pepper. Mince the red onion, cut the jalapeño pepper in half to reduce heat, and finely slice the fresh cilantro.
3. Stir the Ingredients: In a bowl, mix the diced mangoes, red bell pepper, chopped red onion, minced jalapeño, and chopped cilantro.
4. Sugar and Lime Juice: Top the mango mixture with the juice from two limes.
5. You may add a spoonful of honey or agave syrup for an extra sweet touch. The maturity of the mangoes should be considered while adjusting the sweetness.
6. Add salt and pepper to the salsa according to your taste. Carefully mix all the ingredients.
7. Optional: Cover the dish and refrigerate the Illuminated Mango Salsa for 30 minutes to let the flavours blend and improve the taste.
8. To serve, spoon or drizzle the Illuminated Mango Salsa over various foods.

- **Indulge:** This mango salsa is a riot of flavour, with tangy, savoury and spicy undertones that will cool you down. It's great on its own or as a dip for tortilla chips or grilled fish. It would be a great addition to a celestial-themed dinner.

NOTE:

- Please feel free to modify the ingredients and the amount of spice to your liking. This vibrant and fragrant salsa combines ripe mangoes, jalapeños, lime, and cilantro and is a perfect complement to your culinary masterpieces because of its sweetness, spice, and freshness.

16. CRESCENT CAULIFLOWER CRUST PIZZA

INGREDIENTS:

- 1 medium head cauliflower, riced
- 1 egg, beaten
- 1/2 cup shredded mozzarella cheese
- 1/4 cup grated Parmesan cheese
- 1 teaspoon dried oregano
- 1/2 teaspoon garlic powder
- Salt and pepper to taste
- Pizza sauce
- Shredded mozzarella cheese
- Toppings of your choice
- Fresh basil leaves for garnish (optional)

INSTRUCTIONS:

1. Prepare the oven for 400°F (200°C) before making the cauliflower rice. Roll out parchment paper to line a baking pan.
2. After floret-cutting the cauliflower, pulse the pieces in a food processor until they look like rice. The recommended amount of cauliflower rice is around 4 cups.
3. Saute the Cauliflower Rice and Set It Aside:
4. To make the cauliflower rice soft, microwave it in a microwave-safe bowl for four to five minutes on high heat.
5. Let the cooked cauliflower rice cool slightly before transferring it to a clean kitchen towel or cheesecloth. Remove excess moisture by squeezing. For a perfectly crisp crust, this is an absolute must.
6. For the cauliflower crust, add the following ingredients to a large bowl: beaten egg, shredded mozzarella, grated Parmesan, dried oregano, garlic powder, salt, and pepper. Mix well. Drain the cauliflower rice. Blend Everything until smooth.
7. Place the cauliflower mixture on the baking sheet that has been preheated. You may make it into a circle or any form you choose for your pizza. A quarter of an inch is the recommended thickness. The crust will be formed by this.
8. The cauliflower crust has to be baked in a preheated oven for twenty to twenty-five minutes or until it becomes brown and feels firm when touched.
9. Put the Pizza Crust Together: Take the cauliflower crust out of the oven. Coat the dough with pizza sauce, leaving a little border around the edges.
10. Sprinkle the sauce with shredded mozzarella cheese
11. before piling on your preferred pizza toppings.

12. Return the pizza to the oven for 10 to 15 minutes after assembling to allow the cheese to melt and bubble.
13. Take the Crescent Cauliflower Crust Pizza out of the oven and top with your garnishes. If you want, you can toss in some fresh basil leaves for garnish.

Cut and Savor:

Savour the flavour of the low-carb cauliflower crust as you slice the pizza into wedges and serve it right away.

TAKE NOTE:

Crescent cauliflower dough is a fantastic alternative to traditional pizza dough if you're watching your carb intake or want to eat more vegetables. Cauliflower pizza with a crunchy crust that you can top anyhow you choose!

17. GLOWING GINGER CARROT SOUP

INGREDIENTS:

- 1 tablespoon olive oil or butter
- 1 onion, chopped
- 2 cloves garlic, minced
- 1 tablespoon fresh ginger, grated
- 1 lb (about 450g) carrots, peeled and chopped
- 4 cups vegetable or chicken broth
- 1 teaspoon ground turmeric
- 1/2 teaspoon ground cumin
- 1/2 teaspoon ground coriander
- 1/4 teaspoon ground cinnamon
- Salt and pepper to taste
- Coconut milk or cream (optional for added creaminess)
- Fresh cilantro or parsley for garnish (optional)

INSTRUCTIONS:

1. In a large saucepan, melt the olive oil or butter over medium heat. Cook the spices and herbs. After the onion has begun to turn translucent, add the chopped onion and continue sautéing.
2. Before adding the grated ginger and minced garlic, simmer for another minute, or until fragrant.
3. Toss in the aromatics and sauté the diced carrots for a quick minute.
4. Before covering the carrots with the vegetable or chicken broth, toss in the spices. Add some seasonings like salt, pepper, cinnamon, cumin, coriander, and ground turmeric.
5. Simmer the ingredients after bringing them to a boil. When carrots are soft, reduce heat and simmer, covered, for 10 to 25 minutes.
6. After cooking the carrots, take the soup pot from the heat and let it cool somewhat before pureeing.
7. To get the silkiest, creamiest texture possible, mix the soup in stages or use an immersion blender.
8. If the soup is too thick, add more broth or water, and adjust the flavor to taste. Adjust the consistency to your liking. Taste and season to taste.
9. You may add a little coconut milk or cream and mix it in for an extra silky texture. Although it is not necessary, this step enhances the soup's flavor.
10. If you feel the soup needs to be reheated, you can do so in a pot on low heat before serving.
11. Before garnishing, fill empty plates with the Glowing Ginger Carrot Soup.

12. To enhance the flavor and color, you can top it with some fresh parsley or cilantro. Enjoy this vibrant and nutritious Glowing Ginger Carrot Soup, which combines the earthy sweetness of carrots with the warmth of ginger and aromatic spices.

NOTE

Taste the soup before serving to determine the desired consistency and ingredients. With some more time on your hands, you could make this soup. Bring this healthy and filling soup to any event, and you'll be the center of attention.

18. RADIATING RASPBERRY OAT BARS

INGREDIENTS:

- 2 cups rolled oats
- 1 cup all-purpose flour
- 1/2 cup brown sugar
- 1/2 teaspoon baking powder
- 1/4 teaspoon salt
- 1/2 cup unsalted butter, melted
- 1 egg, lightly beaten
- 1 teaspoon vanilla extract
- 1 cup raspberry jam or preserves
- Fresh raspberries for garnish (optional)

INSTRUCTIONS:

1. Oven Prep: Set the oven's temperature to 350°F, or 175°C. Grease or line an 8x8-inch or comparable baking pan with parchment paper.
2. Get the oat base ready:
3. The rolled oats, flour, brown sugar, baking powder, and salt should all be combined in a mixing dish.
4. Add the moist ingredients:
5. Add the melted butter, egg, and vanilla essence to the oat mixture while stirring. Combine all of the ingredients and stir until crumbly.
6. Create a Bar Layout: Spread about two-thirds of the oat mixture evenly over the bottom of the prepared baking pan.
7. Spread Raspberry Jam: Leaving a thin border all the way around, evenly spoon raspberry jam over the oat layer.
8. To make the topping, evenly sprinkle the remaining oat mixture over the raspberry jam layer, covering it completely.
9. Bake: In a preheated oven, Bake the baking pan for 25 to 30 minutes, or until the top is golden brown.
10. After cooking, take the pan out of the oven and allow it to cool fully in the pan on a wire rack. Then, slice it.
11. When the bars are cold, carefully remove them from the pan with the help of the parchment paper and place them on a cutting board.
12. Cut the Radiating Raspberry Oat Bars into the desired-sized squares or bars.

13. Garnish (Optional): Consider placing a fresh raspberry on top of each bar for an added taste and decorative element.
14. Present and Savor:
15. Present these charming Radiating Raspberry Oat Bars as a delicious after-meal treat, savouring the richness of the raspberry jam contrasted with the dense oats.

NOTE:

- You may keep these bars for a few days at room temperature if you put them in an airtight container. They are a delicious snack or a sweet touch to an afternoon tea or party with a cosmic theme. Try a variety of fruit preserves or jams to see how the flavours change!

19. LEMON-GARLIC SHRIMP SKEWERS

INGREDIENTS:

- 1 pound large shrimp, peeled and deveined
- 3 cloves garlic, minced
- Zest of 1 lemon
- Juice of 1 lemon
- 3 tablespoons olive oil
- 2 tablespoons fresh parsley, chopped
- Salt and pepper to taste
- Wooden or metal skewers

INSTRUCTIONS:

1. To make the marinade, put the parsley, olive oil, zest, juice, garlic, salt, and pepper in a bowl. Mix thoroughly.
2. Marinate Shrimp: Using paper towels, pat dry the peeled and deveined shrimp to eliminate any remaining moisture.
3. Toss the shrimp in the marinade until they are well covered. Letting the shrimp soak in the marinade at least fifteen to twenty minutes.
4. Get the oven or grill ready: The outdoor barbecue or grill pan temperature should be set to medium-high. If you're cooking in an oven, set the broiler to high heat.
5. Skewer Shrimp: To hold the marinated shrimp in place, thread them onto skewers and pierce through the thickest section of each shrimp.
6. Shrimp on a skewer should be placed on a hot grill or broiler.
7. The shrimp should be cooked on each side for two to three minutes until they are opaque and pink. Don't overcook them to keep them soft.
8. Serve: Take the Lemon-Garlic Shrimp Skewers out of the oven or grill once finished.
9. Garnish (Optional): You can add more chopped parsley and lemon wedges to the shrimp skewers before serving.
10. Have fun:
11. Serve these delectable, freshly grilled Lemon-Garlic Shrimp Skewers as a light snack, a main course, or a great way to kick off a dinner party with a starry theme.

NOTE:

> You are welcome to modify the seasoning to suit your tastes. These shrimp skewers with lemon-garlic deliver a blast of fragrant and acidic tastes, making them ideal for seafood lovers and for whipping up a spicy, fast meal.

20. CRESCENT CUCUMBER CANAPÉS

INGREDIENTS:

- 1 large cucumber
- 4 ounces cream cheese, softened
- 2 tablespoons mayonnaise
- 1/4 teaspoon garlic powder
- 1/4 teaspoon onion powder
- Salt and pepper to taste
- Fresh dill or chives for garnish (optional)

INSTRUCTIONS:

1. Peel and slice the cucumber. Thoroughly wash it and blot it dry with a paper towel. Thinly slice the cucumber lengthwise into quarter-inch rounds.
2. The ingredients for Cream Cheese Spread are mayonnaise, softened cream cheese, onion and garlic powders, salt, and pepper. Mix until smooth and combined.
3. Assemble the appetizers:
4. To completely coat a cucumber slice, spread the cream cheese mixture you just made.
5. Make Crescent Forms:
6. With the cream cheese still distributed inside, gently fold each cucumber slice in half to create a semicircle or crescent shape.
7. Garnish (Optional): Top the Crescent Cucumber Canapés with finely chopped chives or fresh dill for a little more taste and flair.
8. Serve: Place the ready-to-eat canapés on a plate.
9. Enjoy: Present these light and delicious Crescent Cucumber Canapés as a classy start to a dinner party or as a charming complement to a celestial-themed get-together.

NOTE:

- Adding herbs or spices may adjust the cream cheese spread to your taste. These visually stunning canapés have a cold, creamy flavour that makes them ideal as an exquisite appetizer for various situations or as a light, refreshing snack. Personalize the taste profile by adjusting the spice to your liking.

FIRST QUARTER RECIPES:

21. QUARTER MOON QUESADILLAS

INGREDIENTS:

- 4 large flour tortillas
- 2 cups cooked and shredded chicken
- 2 cups shredded cheese
- 1/2 cup diced bell peppers
- 1/4 cup diced red onion
- 1/4 cup chopped fresh cilantro
- 1 teaspoon ground cumin
- 1 teaspoon chilli powder (adjust to taste)
- Salt and pepper to taste
- Olive oil or butter for cooking

INSTRUCTIONS:

1. To make the filling, put the shredded chicken, cheese, diced red onion, diced bell peppers, chopped cilantro, ground cumin, chilli powder, salt, and pepper in a mixing bowl. Toss to blend thoroughly.
2. Put the quesadillas together:
3. Place two flour tortillas face down on a clean surface.
4. Spread the filling mixture equally over half of each tortilla after dividing it between them.
5. Fold and Form the Quarter Moon Shape: To form a half-moon, fold each tortilla in half over the filling.
6. Shape into Quarter Moons: Cut each half-moon-shaped tortilla into quarters with a knife to get four quarter-moon custards.
7. The quesadillas should be cooked in a pan or skillet heated over medium heat with a small amount of butter or olive oil.
8. After placing the quarter-moon quesadillas onto the skillet, cook them on each side for two to three minutes or until the cheese melts and they become golden brown.
9. After cooking, remove the quarter-moon quesadillas from the grill and transfer them to a platter for serving.
10. Optional garnish: Add more fresh cilantro to the dish or serve it with guacamole, sour cream, or salsa on the side for dipping.

11. Enjoy: These tasty and entertaining Quarter Moon Quesadillas are a unique snack or appetizer and are ideal for events with a cosmic theme.

NOTE:

- ➤ You may change the filling components to suit your tastes by substituting various kinds of cheese, adding beans, or varying the spices to create a variety of flavours. These visually stunning and tasty quesadillas in the form of a quarter moon are a terrific way to add a celestial touch to your meals.

22. STELLAR SESAME NOODLE SALAD

INGREDIENTS:

- 8 ounces (about 225g) noodles of your choice
- 1/4 cup soy sauce
- 3 tablespoons sesame oil
- 2 tablespoons rice vinegar
- 2 tablespoons honey or brown sugar
- 2 cloves garlic, minced
- 1 tablespoon fresh ginger, grated
- 1 tablespoon sesame seeds and plus more for garnish
- 1 tablespoon green onions (scallions), chopped (optional)
- 1 cup shredded carrots
- 1 cup cucumber, julienned or thinly sliced
- 1/4 cup diced fresh cilantro or parsley for garnish

INSTRUCTIONS:

1. Prepare Noodles: Prepare the noodles as directed on the box. To stop the cooking process, drain the cooked noodles and rinse them under cold water. Set aside.
2. Get the dressing ready:
3. Combine soy sauce, sesame oil, rice vinegar, honey or brown sugar, grated ginger, chopped garlic, and sesame seeds in a mixing bowl and whisk until thoroughly blended.
4. Ingredients: Combine the shredded carrots, cucumber slices, and cooked, chilled noodles in a large mixing dish.
5. Include Dressing:
6. Drizzle the prepared dressing over the noodle and veggie combination. Gently toss to distribute the dressing throughout.
7. Chill (optional): To bring out the flavours in the Stellar Sesame Noodle Salad, cover it and place it in the refrigerator for around half an hour.
8. Garnish and Serve: Sprinkle the noodle salad with more sesame seeds, finely chopped fresh cilantro or parsley, and diced green onions, if used, as soon as it's cold (if preferred).
9. Have fun:
10. Serve this tasty and light Stellar Sesame Noodle Salad as an appetizer or a side dish. It's a great way to kick off a celestial-themed event or to pair it with your favourite main courses.

NOTE:

- Add other ingredients, like sliced bell peppers, edamame, or tofu, to add texture and taste. Adjust the dressing's sweetness or amount of spice. This salad tastes best when eaten right away. However, it may also be stored in the refrigerator to enhance the flavour over time.

23. LUMINARY LEMON CHICKEN

INGREDIENTS:

- 4 boneless, skinless chicken breasts
- 1/4 cup all-purpose flour
- Salt and pepper to taste
- 2 tablespoons olive oil
- 4 cloves garlic, minced
- 1/2 cup chicken broth
- 1/4 cup fresh lemon juice
- Zest of 1 lemon
- 2 tablespoons unsalted butter
- 2 tablespoons fresh parsley, chopped (for garnish)
- Lemon slices for garnish (optional)

INSTRUCTIONS:

1. Chicken preparation: Pat the chicken breasts dry with paper towels. After lightly dredging each breast in flour and brushing off any excess, season them with salt and pepper.
2. To sear the chicken, place a large pan over medium-high heat with olive oil. When the chicken breasts are golden brown and well cooked, add them to the skillet and boil for about 4–5 minutes on each side. After removing it from the pan, set the chicken aside.
3. In the same skillet, sauté the minced garlic for about a minute over medium heat, or until fragrant, to produce the lemon sauce.
4. After adding the lemon juice, zest, and chicken stock, scrape away any browned pieces from the pan's bottom.
5. Simmer the liquid for two to three minutes to slightly decrease it.
6. Put in the butter, and finish the sauce by turning down the heat. When the unsalted butter melts and blends with the sauce to form a smooth consistency, add it to the skillet and stir.
7. Return the chicken to the pan. Spoon the lemon sauce over the cooked chicken breasts before placing them back in the pan. Drizzle some sauce on the poultry.
8. Simmer and Garnish: Simmer the chicken for two to three more minutes or until it's well-cooked and covered in the delicious sauce.
9. If preferred, garnish with slices of lemon and freshly cut parsley.
10. Serve: Drizzle the delectable lemon sauce over the hot Luminary Lemon Chicken.
11. Have fun:
12. Savour the flavour of succulent, juicy chicken breasts dipped in a zesty lemon-infused sauce with this vibrant, zesty Luminary Lemon Chicken.

NOTE:
- For a more or less sour flavor, you can adjust the quantity of lemon juice according to your preference. Rice, spaghetti, steamed vegetables, or a fresh salad are all great accompaniments to this dish. The vibrant colors and flavor of this chicken dish will make your meal taste even better.

24. RADIANT ROASTED VEGGIES

INGREDIENTS:

Assorted vegetables of your choice, such as:

- 2 cups broccoli florets
- 2 cups cauliflower florets
- 1 large bell pepper, sliced
- 1 medium zucchini, sliced
- 1 medium yellow squash, sliced
- 1 red onion, sliced
- Cherry tomatoes (optional)
- 3 tablespoons olive oil
- 2-3 cloves garlic, minced
- 1 teaspoon dried herbs (such as rosemary, and thyme, or Italian seasoning)
- Salt and pepper to taste
- Fresh herbs

INSTRUCTION:

1. Place the oven on 425 degrees Fahrenheit (220 degrees Celsius). To make cleaning easier, line a large baking sheet with parchment paper or aluminum foil.
2. Get the veggies ready.
3. Please ensure the mixed veggies are around the same size throughout, even for cooking,g as you wash and cut them into bite-sized chunks or slices.
4. Combine all the veggies in a big mixing basin and toss them with olive oil, minced garlic, dry herbs, salt, and pepper. Make sure the spice mixture coats the vegetables evenly.
5. Arrange on Baking Sheet: Make sure the seasoned veggies are not packed too tightly by spreading them out in a single layer on the baking sheet or pan that has been preheated. If more baking sheets are required, use them.
6. Preheat the oven to 400 degrees. Once the oven is hot, put the baking sheet in the middle and roast the vegetables for 20 to 25 minutes, or until they are tender and starting to turn a golden color. To make sure they brown evenly, toss them halfway through.
7. After finishing, take the Radiant Roasted Veggies out of the oven, garnish and serve.
8. If desired, garnish with fresh herbs.
9. Have fun:
10. Serve these colorful and tasty radiant-roasted veggies as a filler for wraps, sandwiches, pasta dishes, and grain bowls or as a healthful side dish.

NOTE:

- You are welcome to alter the vegetable choices according to your tastes or the produce in season. Vegetables take on a natural sweetness and taste that is enhanced by roasting. Not only are these roasted vegetables tasty, but they can be used as a stand-alone dish or a great way to add colour and nutrients to various meals. To suit your tastes, adjust the herbs and seasoning.

25. LUNAR LENTIL LOAF

INGREDIENTS:

- 2 cups cooked green or brown lentils
- 1 onion, finely chopped
- 2 cloves garlic, minced
- 1 carrot, grated
- 1 celery stalk, finely chopped
- 1 bell pepper (any colour), finely chopped
- 1 cup breadcrumbs (or rolled oats for a gluten-free option)
- 1/2 cup tomato sauce or ketchup
- 2 tablespoons soy sauce or tamari
- 2 tablespoons Worcestershire sauce (optional)
- 2 tablespoons olive oil
- 1 teaspoon dried thyme
- 1 teaspoon dried oregano
- 1/2 teaspoon paprika
- Salt and pepper to taste
- Cooking spray or olive oil for greasing

INSTRUCTIONS:

1. Oven Prep: Set the oven's temperature to 375°F, or 190°C. Apply cooking spray or olive oil to a loaf pan.
2. Mix the lentils.
3. Mash cooked lentil
4. s with a fork or potato masher in a large bowl until almost mashed but remaining chunky.
5. To sauté vegetables, place a pan over medium heat with olive oil. Add the bell pepper, diced onion, minced garlic, grated carrot, and chopped celery. Vegetables should be sautéed for five to seven minutes to soften them. Take it off the fire and let it cool a little.
6. Combine Ingredients: Add the sautéed veggies, rolled oats or breadcrumbs, tomato sauce, ketchup, soy sauce, Worcestershire sauce (if using), paprika, dried thyme, dried oregano, and salt and pepper to the mashed lentils. Mix well until all components are correctly incorporated.
7. Shape the Loaf:
8. Using a spatula to level the surface, press down firmly and transfer the lentil mixture into the buttered loaf pan.
9. Bake the Lunar Lentil Loaf for 40 to 45 minutes, or until the top is solid and beginning to crisp up, by placing the loaf pan in the preheated oven.

10. After baking, take the lentil loaf out of the oven and rest in the pan for ten minutes before slicing.

Cut and Savor:

1. Serve the warm Lunar Lentil Loaf with your preferred sides, gravy, or sauce after carefully slicing it.

NOTE:

- As a tasty and healthy substitute for classic meatloaf, try this Lunar Lentil Loaf. Feel free to change the seasonings and add more herbs or spices to suit your tastes. This recipe with a cosmic theme is a fantastic choice for any event or dinner. It is filling and suitable for vegetarians and lovers of lentils.

26. QUARTER PHASE QUINOA PILAF

INGREDIENTS:

- 1 cup quinoa, rinsed thoroughly
- 2 cups vegetable or chicken broth
- 1 tablespoon olive oil
- 1 small onion, finely chopped
- 2 cloves garlic, minced
- 1 bell pepper (any colour), diced
- 1 carrot, diced
- 1 zucchini, diced
- 1/2 cup frozen peas
- 1 teaspoon ground cumin
- 1 teaspoon paprika
- To taste, add salt and pepper.
- For garnish, cut some fresh cilantro or parsley (optional).

INSTRUCTIONS:

1. Rinse Quinoa: Run cold water through a fine-mesh strainer over the quinoa to get rid of any bitterness. Make sure to drain thoroughly.
2. After washing, put the quinoa in a saucepan and cook it with water, vegetable broth, or chicken stock. Reduce the heat to a simmer and let the quinoa come to a boil. Cover and cook the quinoa for 15 to 20 minutes or until it softens and the liquid is completely absorbed. Fluff with a fork and put aside.
3. Sauté vegetables: Heat olive oil in a big skillet or frying pan over medium heat. Add chopped onion and cook until transparent, two to three minutes.
4. Add the minced garlic, diced bell pepper, chopped carrot, and diced zucchini to the pan. Stirring periodically, sauté the veggies for five to seven minutes more, or until they start to soften slightly.
5. Quinoa and veggies Together: Put the cooked quinoa and the sautéed veggies in a pan. Toss to blend thoroughly.
6. Mix in the ground cumin, paprika, frozen peas, salt, and pepper to season the pilaf. Simmer the peas for two to three minutes to enable the flavours to combine and the peas to reheat.

7. Finish and Serve: Turn off the heat when finished. Add some finely chopped fresh parsley or cilantro to the Quarter Phase Quinoa Pila if preferred.
8. Enjoy: Serve this tasty and healthy Quarter Phase Quinoa Pilaf as a light main course or as a side dish with your favourite protein. You can even serve it as a dinner inspired by the stars.

NOTE:

Feel free to add more veggies or herbs to improve the taste. This is an adaptable, nutrient-dense quinoa pilaf that you can simply tailor to your tastes. It's a fantastic way to include quinoa and other vibrant veggies in your meals.

27. SPARKLING STRAWBERRY SALAD

INGREDIENTS:

- 6 cups mixed salad greens (spinach, arugula, or lettuce)
- 2 cups fresh strawberries, hulled and sliced
- Half a cup of shredded goat or feta cheese
- 1/4 cup candied pecans or sliced almonds
- 1/4 cup finely sliced red onion
- For the Dressing:
- 3 tablespoons balsamic vinegar
- 2 tablespoons honey or maple syrup
- 1/4 cup extra-virgin olive oil
- Salt and pepper to taste

INSTRUCTIONS:

1. To prepare the salad greens, wash and dry them thoroughly. Transfer them to a large salad bowl.
2. Cut up the red onion and strawberries:
3. Cut the fresh strawberries into halves. Cut the red onion thinly.
4. Put Salad Together:
5. In the salad bowl with the greens, toss in the sliced almonds or candied pecans, sliced red onion, crumbled goat cheese or feta, and sliced strawberries
6. Get the dressing ready:"To make the dressing, mix extra virgin olive oil,
7. balsamic vinegar, honey, salt, and pepper in a small bowl.
8. Once done, transfer the Sparkling Strawberry Salad to a salad bowl or serving plates for serving."
9. Enjoy: This colourful and crisp Sparkling Strawberry Salad is perfect as a side dish or a lovely snack. It highlights the sweetness of the strawberries, the tanginess of the dressing and the savoury flavour of the cheese and nuts.

NOTE:

> You may alter this salad by adding extras like avocado slices, grilled ChickenChicken, or fresh herbs like mint or basil. This adaptable salad perfectly encapsulates the crispness and delectability of strawberries, making it ideal for entertaining in the spring or summer or serving as a vibrant and refreshing side dish for any meal. Modify the dressing components to your tastes to get the perfect flavour balance.

28. LUNAR ECLIPSE EMPANADAS

INGREDIENTS:

For the Dough:

- 2 1/2 cups all-purpose flour
- 1/2 teaspoon salt
- 1/2 cup unsalted butter (cold), cut into cubes
- 1 egg
- 1/3 cup cold water
- 1 tablespoon white vinegar or lemon juice

For the Filling:

- 2 tablespoons olive oil
- 1 onion, finely chopped
- 2 cloves garlic, minced
- 1 bell pepper (any colour), finely diced
- 1 cup cooked and shredded ChickenChicken or beef (or a vegetarian alternative like black beans or lentils)
- 1/2 cup frozen corn kernels
- 1/2 cup black olives, sliced
- 1 teaspoon ground cumin
- 1 teaspoon paprika
- To taste, add salt and pepper.
- 1/4 cups of freshly chopped parsley [or cilantro]
- Half a cup of shredded cheese (either mozzarella, Monterey Jack, or cheddar)

INSTRUCTIONS:

Mix the salt, flour in a bowl to form the dough. Combine all ingredients by stirring.

1. Using your hands or a pastry cutter, cut the cold butter into the dough until it resembles coarse crumbs.
2. Whisk the egg, lemon juice, and white vinegar in a different small dish. Stir the whisking ingredients into the dough just until it begins to come together. Refrigerate the dough for a minimum of thirty minutes after rolling it into a ball and covering it with plastic wrap.
3. In a skillet over medium heat, warm the olive oil to prepare the filling. When the onions are translucent, add them and sauté.
4. Add chopped bell pepper and minced garlic and sauté for two to three more minutes.
5. Then, add cooked or shredded beef, chicken, or vegetarian substitute, frozen corn kernels, chopped black olives, paprika, ground cumin, salt, and pepper. Cook until the flavors are blended and the mixture is thoroughly cooked, then simmer it for five to seven minutes. After removing it from the heat source, add chopped parsley or cilantro. Allow the filling to cool.
6. Fold the empanadas in half and bake them at 375°F (190°C) on a baking sheet lined with parchment paper.
7. On a surface dusted with flour, roll out the cold dough to a thickness of about 1/8 inch. Cut circles out of paper using a circular cutter that has a diameter of about 5 to 6 inches.
8. Finish and Close: Make sure that each dough circle has a dollop of the chilled filling in the middle. Cover the filling with a layer of shredded cheese.
9. A fork should be used to seal the edges after folding the dough over the filling to form a half-moon.
10. Place the empanadas on the baking sheet that has been prepped for baking. If you want a golden finish, you can brush the tops with beaten egg.
11. Preheat the oven and bake the empanadas for 20 to 25 minutes or until they are golden brown. Remove the Lunar Eclipse Empanadas from the oven and serve immediately after baking. Allow it to cool a little before serving.
12. Serve these delicious empanadas as an appetizer, a snack, or a part of a starry-themed dinner.

NOTE:

- Because empanadas are so adaptable, you may change the ingredients in the filling to fit your dietary needs or taste preferences. These tasty pastries provide a delicious and portable snack that will please any crowd, making them ideal for parties or get-togethers. Tailor the spices and fillings to your unique preferences.

29. SIZZLIN' STEAK STIR-FRY

INGREDIENTS:

- 1 pound flank steak, sirloin steak, or beef of your choice, thinly sliced against the grain
- 2 tablespoons soy sauce
- 2 tablespoons oyster sauce
- 1 tablespoon hoisin sauce
- 1 tablespoon cornstarch
- 2 tablespoons vegetable oil (divided)
- 3 cloves garlic, minced
- 1-inch piece of ginger, minced or grated
- 1 red bell pepper, sliced
- 1 green bell pepper, sliced
- 1 yellow bell pepper, sliced
- 1 sliced onion
- 1 cup florets of broccoli
- 1 cup sugar snap peas or snap peas
- Salt and pepper to taste
- Cooked rice or noodles for serving

INSTRUCTIONS:

1. Marinate the Steak: Put the thinly sliced steak, oyster sauce, hoisin sauce, and cornstarch in a basin. Thoroughly mix to evenly cover the steak. Leave it to marinate for fifteen to twenty minutes.
2. Get the veggies ready:
3. Dice the onion and bell peppers. Chop broccoli into small pieces. Clean and cut snap peas.
4. Stir-fry: Heat 1 tablespoon of vegetable oil over high heat in a big pan or wok. Cook the marinated steak for two to three minutes on each side, or until browned, by adding it in a single layer. After taking the meat from the grill, set it aside.
5. Get the veggies ready: Add the last tablespoon of oil to the same wok or pan. Stir-fry the ginger and garlic until aromatic, which should take around 30 seconds.
6. Add the onion, snap peas, broccoli florets, and sliced bell peppers. The veggies should be crisp and tender after 4–5 minutes of sautéing.
7. Taste
8. and Combination: Return the cooked meat and veggies to the skillet. Stir everything and simmer for one or two minutes to bring it all up to temperature.
9. Put the flour and salt in a bowl and whisk to fully incorporate to produce the dough.
10. Serve the Sizzlin' Steak Stir-Fry with noodles or boiled rice on the side.

11. Have fun: Savour this aromatic and spicy stir-fry for a filling supper ideal for a quick and tasty dinner.

NOTE:

- You may change the veggies in the stir-fry depending on your tastes or what's in season. This dish is a good choice for a full and enjoyable supper since it delivers a nice blend of tender beef, crisp veggies, and savoury spices. Adjust the cooking time depending on how well done you want the steak and veggies to be.

30. BRILLIANT BARLEY BOWL

INGREDIENTS:

- 1 cup pearl barley, rinsed
- Two and a half cups of water or vegetable or chicken broth
- 2 tablespoons olive oil
- 1 onion, finely chopped
- 2 cloves garlic, minced
- 1 red bell pepper, diced
- 1 yellow bell pepper, diced
- 1 cup cherry tomatoes, halved
- 1 cup cooked chickpeas (canned, drained and rinsed)
- 2 cups baby spinach or kale, chopped
- 1/4 cup chopped fresh parsley
- Juice of 1 lemon
- Salt and pepper to taste
- Optional toppings: crumbled feta cheese, avocado slices, toasted nuts or seeds

INSTRUCTIONS:

1. After giving the barley a good rinse, add water, vegetable broth, or chicken broth to a medium pot. Be careful not to boil. After the barley boils, After the liquid has evaporated, reduce heat to a simmer, cover, and cook for 30–40 minutes, or until tender. Once the barley has cooked, fluff it slightly with a fork and put it aside.
2. Gather all of the vegetables and lentils.
3. While the barley cooks, place a large skillet over medium heat with the olive oil. When translucent, add the onion and simmer for a further two to three minutes.
4. To the skillet, add the diced bell peppers and minced garlic. When the peppers begin to soften, add them and continue cooking for another three to four minutes.
5. Add the cooked chickpeas and cherry tomatoes, and simmer for two to three minutes or until the tomatoes soften.
6. Mix BarleyBarley with veggies: Put the cooked BarleyBarley, chickpeas, and sautéed veggies in a pan. Toss to thoroughly mix in all the ingredients.
7. Add Baby Spinach or Kale and Seasoning: Add the chopped greens to the skillet, toss until they wilt, and mix in with the other ingredients.
8. Drizzle the barley dish with lemon juice. Season with salt and pepper to taste. Add freshly cut parsley and mix.
9. Serve: Distribute the Brilliant Barley Bowl among bowls for serving.

10. Enjoy: To enhance the taste and texture, sprinkle feta cheese crumbles, avocado slices, toasted almonds, or sesame seeds on top of each bowl.
11. Enjoy: Great for lunch or supper, this colourful and nutrient-dense Brilliant Barley Bowl makes a fulfilling meal.

NOTE:

> This is a very flexible dish that you can alter to suit your tastes by substituting different veggies or types of protein. Barley is an excellent foundation for a filling bowl because of its chewy texture and nutty flavour. To add a unique touch and taste and adjust the flavour and garnishes.

WAXING GIBBOUS RECIPES:

31. LUMINOUS LEMON BARS

INGREDIENTS:

For the Crust:

- 1 1/2 cups all-purpose flour
- 1/2 cup confectioners' sugar
- 3/4 cup unsalted butter, softened

For the Lemon Filling:

- 4 large eggs
- 1 1/2 cups granulated sugar
- 1/4 cup all-purpose flour
- Zest of 2 lemons
- 3/4 cups fresh lemon juice (about 4-5 lemons)
- Confectioners' sugar for dusting

INSTRUCTIONS:

1. Oven Prep: Set the oven's temperature to 350°F, or 175°C. A 9 x 13-inch baking dish should be greased or lined with parchment paper, providing an overhang for simple removal.
2. Get the crust ready:
3. Mix the flour, softened butter, and confectioners' sugar in a mixing basin until the mixture resembles coarse crumbs.
4. In the bottom of the baking dish that has been prepared, press the batter evenly.
5. Once the oven is warmed, the crust should be lightly browned, which should take around 18 to 20 minutes. After taking it out of the oven, put it aside.
6. Gather the flour, eggs, granulated sugar, lemon zest, and fresh lemon juice in a separate
7. basin. Whisk until completely incorporated. This is the Lemon Filling.Cooking and Scattering: Spoon the lemon filling over the pre-baked crust.
8. After 20–25 minutes, or until the filling has set and the sides are starting to brown a little, put the baking dish back in the oven.
9. Let the Luminous Lemon Bars cool thoroughly in the baking dish at room temperature before chilling them. To set and firm up, relax in the refrigerator for at least two hours after cooling.

10. Cut and Dust: After cooling and solidifying the bars, cut them into squares or rectangles with a sharp knife.
11. Sprinkle confectioners' sugar over the tops right before serving.
12. Indulge and Enjoy: These Luminous Lemon Bars are a gorgeous and zingy dessert option.

NOTE:
- To produce clean, tidy squares, ensure the lemon bars are well cold and thoroughly cooled before slicing. These lemon bars are sweet and tart and ideal as a dessert for get-togethers or parties or as a tasty snack with tea or coffee. Adjust the amount dependingAdjust the amount depending on how sweet you want your confectioners' sugar to be.

32. HOMEMADE GRANOLA BARS

INGREDIENTS:

- ❖ 2 cups rolled oats
- ❖ 1/2 cup nuts or seeds (almonds, walnuts, pumpkin seeds, etc.), chopped
- ❖ 1/2 cup dried fruits (raisins, cranberries, chopped apricots, etc.)
- ❖ 1/4 cup honey or maple syrup
- ❖ 1/4 cups peanut butter or almond butter
- ❖ 1 teaspoon vanilla extract
- ❖ 1/4 teaspoon salt
- ❖ Optional: chocolate chips, coconut flakes, cinnamon, etc.

INSTRUCTIONS:

1. Preheat oven to 175°C/350°F. Dry components can be saved. Oil and paper an 8x8 baking dish.
2. Mix rolled oats, chopped nuts or seeds, and dried fruits in a big bowl.
3. Make Granola Bars:
4. Heat honey or maple syrup in a skillet over low heat and mix in almond or peanut butter until smooth. Add vanilla essence and salt to the skillet after turning off.
5. Mix syrup or honey with dry ingredients in a bowl. Mix until all dry components are incorporated.
6. In baking dish Press:
7. Put the mixture in the baking dish. Press it evenly into the dish using a spatula or spoon.
8. Pre-heat the
9. oven and bake the bars for 20–25 minutes until golden brown.
10. Allow granola bars to cool fully in the baking dish before slicing. After granola cools, remove parchment paper and place slab on cutting board. Cut squares or bars to size.
11. In an airtight container, homemade granola bars can be kept at room temperature for a week. Wrap each one individually for portable munching.

NOTE:

> You can adjust these granola bars to your taste by adding chocolate chips, coconut flakes, or other ingredients. They are a healthier option than store-bought ones. They won't glow in the dark, but they will satiate your need for a snack!

33. RADIANT RAMEN BOWL

INGREDIENTS:

- 4 packs of ramen noodles
- 6 cups vegetable broth or chicken broth
- 2 tablespoons sesame oil
- 4 cloves garlic, minced
- 1 tablespoon fresh ginger, grated
- 1 cup sliced shiitake mushrooms
- 1 cup sliced bok choy or spinach
- 1 cup thinly sliced carrots
- 1 cup thinly sliced bell peppers
- 1 cup firm tofu, cubed (optional)
- 2 tablespoons soy sauce
- 1 tablespoon rice vinegar
- 2 teaspoons sriracha sauce or chilli paste (adjust to taste)
- Sliced green onions for garnish
- Sesame seeds for garnish
- Soft-boiled eggs, halved (optional)

INSTRUCTIONS:

1. Prepare the Ramen Noodles: Follow the directions on the package to cook the ramen noodles. Drain and set aside.
2. Get the broth ready:
3. Sesame oil should be heated over medium heat in a big saucepan. Add grated ginger and minced garlic and heat for one minute until fragrant.
4. After adding the vegetable or chicken broth, boil the mixture.
5. Tofu and Vegetables: Add the cubed tofu (if using), sliced bell peppers, bok choy or spinach, sliced carrots, and sliced shiitake mushrooms to the boiling stock. Simmer the veggies for five to seven minutes or until soft but crunchy.
6. Spice up the broth:
7. Add rice vinegar, sriracha sauce, chilli paste, and soy sauce. Taste and adjust the seasoning.
8. Put Ramen Bowls Together:
9. Spoon cooked ramen noodles into individual serving dishes.
10. Spoon the broth and vegetable/tofu mixture over the noodles in each bowl.
11. Garnish and Serve: Sprinkle sesame seeds, sliced green onions, and soft-boiled egg halves (if using) on top of each Radiant Ramen Bowl.
12. Have fun:

13. Enjoy this hearty and tasty lunch by immediately serving the Radiant Ramen Bowls hot.

NOTE:
- ➢ Feel free to alter this recipe by adding or removing veggies and protein sources to suit your tastes. You may also adjust the heat by adjusting the amount of chilli paste or sriracha sauce used. Especially on chilly days or when you want something warm and cosy, these dazzling ramen bowls are adaptable, wholesome, and ideal for a filling dinner.

34. GIBBOUS MOON GARLIC BREAD

INGREDIENTS:

- 1 large French baguette or Italian bread loaf
- 1/2 cup unsalted butter, softened
- 4 cloves garlic, minced
- 2 tablespoons fresh parsley, finely chopped
- 1/4 teaspoon salt
- 1/4 teaspoon black pepper
- 1/2 cup grated Parmesan cheese (optional)

INSTRUCTIONS:

1. Oven Prep: Set the oven's temperature to 375°F, or 190°C.
2. To make the garlic butter mixture, place melted butter, minced garlic, freshly chopped parsley, black pepper, and salt in a small bowl. Mix thoroughly until all components are combined.
3. The French baguette or Italian bread loaf should be sliced lengthwise without cutting through to keep the pieces together.
4. Spread garlic butter evenly across the bread's sliced sides, getting into all the cracks.
5. (Optional) foil wrap: The baked bread can be carefully covered in aluminum foil.
6. Gibbous Moon Garlic Bread should be baked on a baking sheet for 12–15 minutes in a preheated oven until the butter melts and seeps in.
7. Optional Topping: Sprinkle Parmesan cheese on garlic bread in the last two to three minutes of baking. Melting the cheese turns the bread light golden.
8. Slice and Serve: Let Gibbous Moon Garlic Bread cool for a minute or two before cutting. Slice the heated bread into pieces.
9. Have fun:
10. Savour this tasty snack or side dish, Gibbous Moon Garlic Bread.

NOTE:

> This garlic bread is a great, easy snack or side dish for many dinners. You may vary the amount of parsley or garlic to suit your tastes. Extra taste is added using Parmesan cheese, but you can leave it out if you'd rather. To get the crispiness you like, adjust the baking time.

35. ENCHANTED EGGPLANT PARMESAN

INGREDIENTS:

- 2 large eggplants, sliced into 1/2-inch rounds
- 2 cups breadcrumbs (Panko or regular)
- 1 cup grated Parmesan cheese
- 4 eggs, beaten
- 2 cups marinara sauce
- 2 cups shredded mozzarella cheese
- Fresh basil leaves for garnish
- Salt and pepper to taste
- Olive oil for frying

INSTRUCTIONS:

1. To prepare the eggplant, preheat your oven to 190°C, or 375°F. Place eggplant slices on a paper-towel-lined baking pan. Let each slice lie for 15–20 minutes after salting both sides. This reduces moisture. Pat eggplant slices dry with paper towels.
2. Coat eggplant slices: Put breadcrumbs and Parmesan in a shallow dish. Cover both sides of each eggplant slice with breadcrumbs after dipping in beaten eggs.
3. Fry Eggplant: Heat olive oil in a large pan on medium-high. After heating, add the coated eggplant slices in batches and cook for two to three minutes each side until golden brown. Drain oil by placing cooked slices on a paper towel-lined plate.
4. Complete the Plate:Lay marinara sauce on the bottom of a baking dish. Layer sauce-covered fried eggplant slices. Finish with shredded mozzarella and additional marinara sauce on the eggplant. Finish with mozzarella cheese and marinara sauce.
5. Bake: Bake until cheese is bubbling and melted in a preheated oven for 25–30 minutes under foil.
6. Garnish and Serve: Remove the foil and broil the cheese for two to three more minutes until bubbly and golden.
7. Add fresh basil leaves to Enchanted Eggplant Parmesan just before serving.
8. Have fun:
9. Serve pasta or a fresh salad with this delicious Enchanted Eggplant Parmesan main meal.

NOTE:

- This recipe is a tasty vegetarian alternative that returns memories of traditional Italian eggplant parmesan. To suit your tastes, add or subtract spice from the marinara sauce. You may even mix in more Italian herbs or spices with the breadcrumbs for added flavour.

36. BRILLIANT BANANA BREAD

INGREDIENTS:

- 2 to 3 ripe bananas and mashed
- 1/3 cup unsalted butter, melted
- 3/4 cup granulated sugar
- 1 large egg, beaten
- 1 teaspoon vanilla extract
- 1 1/2 cups all-purpose flour
- 1 teaspoon baking soda
- 1/4 teaspoon salt
- 1/2 teaspoon ground cinnamon
- 1/2 cup chopped nuts

INSTRUCTIONS:

1. Preheat oven to 350°F/175°C. Parchment or grease a 9x5-inch loaf pan.
2. Make the Wet Ingredients: Make smooth mashed ripe bananas with a fork in a bowl. Mix melted butter thoroughly.
3. The banana mixture needs vanilla, beaten egg, and granulated sugar. Mix thoroughly.
4. Mix the dry ingredients.
5. A separate bowl should include all-purpose flour, baking soda, salt, and ground cinnamon (if used).
6. Blend dry and wet ingredients:
7. Gently stir dry ingredients into wet until just combined. A few lumps are
8. OK; don't overmix.
9. Add chocolate chips or almonds to the batter.
10. Pour Batter: Pour banana bread batter evenly into the prepared loaf pan.
11. A toothpick put into the center of the loaf pan should come out clean or with a few damp crumbs after 50–60 minutes in the preheated oven.
12. Serve banana bread after 10–15 minutes of pan cooling.
13. Slice bread after cooling on a wire rack.
14. Slice the bread after cooling on a wire rack.
15. Have fun: Cut into pieces and serve the Ingenious Banana Bread as a tasty breakfast or snack.

NOTE:

- You may alter this brilliant banana bread by adding chocolate chips, dried fruits, or nuts like pecans or walnuts to add more texture and taste. To ensure the finest flavour in the bread, make sure your bananas are ripe. Any leftovers can be frozen for prolonged storage or kept for several days at room temperature in an airtight container.

37. LUNAR LAVENDER LATTE

INGREDIENTS:

- 1 cup milk (dairy or non-dairy)
- 1 tablespoon dried culinary lavender buds
- 1 teaspoon honey or sweetener of choice (adjust to taste)
- 1-2 espresso shots or 1/2 cup strong coffee
- Optional: Lavender syrup for added flavour

INSTRUCTIONS:

1. Preheat oven to 350°F/175°C. Prepare a 9x5 loaf pan with paper or oil.
2. Prepare Wet Ingredients: Mash ripe bananas in a bowl with a fork. Add melted butter and mix well.
3. Egg, vanilla, and granulated sugar to banana mixture. Mix well.
4. Mix the dry ingredients:
5. Mix all-purpose flour, baking soda, salt, and ground cinnamon in a separate basin.
6. Dry-Wet Mixture Integration:
7. Only barely combine dry and wet ingredients. Avoid overmixing—a few lumps are OK.
8. Include
9. chocolate chips or chopped almonds in the batter.
10. Pour batter in pan: Put banana bread batter in the loaf pan evenly.
11. Bake: Bake the loaf pan for 50 to 60 Minutes in preheated oven until a toothpick inserted into the middle comes out clean.
12. Serve banana bread 10–15 minutes after pan cooling.
13. Slice bread after wire-rack chilling.
14. Have fun:Cut into pieces and serve the Ingenious Banana Bread as a tasty breakfast or snack.

NOTE:

- You may alter this brilliant banana bread by adding chocolate chips, dried fruits, or nuts like pecans or walnuts to add more texture and taste. To ensure the finest flavour in the bread, make sure your bananas are ripe. Any leftovers can be frozen for prolonged storag, or kept for several days at room temperature in an airtight container.

38. GLOWING GREEN GODDESS SALAD

INGREDIENTS:

For the Salad:

- 4 cups mixed greens (spinach, kale, arugula, etc.)
- 1 cucumber, thinly sliced
- 1 avocado, sliced or diced
- 1 cup snap peas, trimmed and halved
- 1/2 cup broccoli florets, blanched
- 1/4 cup fresh basil leaves, torn
- 1/4 cup fresh mint leaves, torn
- 1/4 cup sunflower or pumpkin seeds
- Optional: Crumbled feta or goat cheese: 1/4 cup

For the Green Goddess Dressing:

- 1/2 cup plain Greek yoghurt or sour cream
- 1/4 cup mayonnaise
- 2 tablespoons chopped fresh parsley
- 2 tablespoons chopped fresh chives
- 1 tablespoon chopped fresh tarragon (optional)
- 1 clove garlic, minced
- 2 tablespoons lemon juices
- 1tbsp cider or white wine vinegar
- Salt and pepper to taste
- Water (to thin dressing, if needed)

INSTRUCTIONS:

1. To make the salad, put the mixed greens, sliced cucumber, avocado, snap peas, blanched broccoli florets, shredded basil and mint leaves, and either pumpkin or sunflower seeds in a large bowl. If preferred, top with crumbled goat or feta cheese.
2. Prepare the Goddess Dressing (Green):
3. A blender or food processor should incorporate Greek yoghurt or sour cream, mayonnaise, chopped parsley, chives, tarragon (if used), minced garlic, lemon juice, white wine or cider vinegar, salt, pepper.
4. Blend until smooth. Dilute thick dressing with a little water to get the correct consistency.
5. Pour Green Goddess Dressing over the salad or serve it separately. Stir the salad gently to coat all parts with dressing.

6. Serve: Arrange the Bright Green Goddess Salad onto a plate or in separate dishes.
7. Have fun:
8. Savour this colourful and nutrient-dense Glowing Green Goddess Salad as a wonderful side dish or a light and healthy dinner.

NOTE:

> ➢ Remember that you can customize this salad to your liking by adding or removing any greens, veggies, nuts, or seeds. You can keep the tasty Green Goddess Dressing in the fridge for a few days. Adjust the dressing's herbs and spices to suit your taste.

39. LUMINESCENT LEMON PEPPER CHICKEN

INGREDIENTS:

- 4 boneless, skinless chicken breasts
- 2 tablespoons olive oil
- Zest of 1-2 lemons
- Juice of 1-2 lemons
- 2 cloves garlic, minced
- 1 teaspoon black pepper (adjust to taste)
- 1 teaspoon salt (adjust to taste)
- 1 teaspoon paprika
- 1 teaspoon dried thyme or rosemary
- 2 tablespoons unsalted butter (optional)
- Fresh parsley for garnish (optional)

INSTRUCTIONS:

1. To prepare the chicken, pat dry the breasts using paper towels. This improves the seasoning's adhesion.
2. Prepare the chicken by marinating it:
3. Combine the olive oil, dried thyme or rosemary, minced garlic, lemon zest, lemon juice, black pepper, and salt in a bowl.
4. Rub the marinade mixture evenly on the chicken breasts to ensure they are well covered. Refrigerate the marinated food for at least 30 minutes to blend flavors.
5. Prepare the Chicken:
6. Over medium-high heat, preheat a skillet or pan. If required, add a small amount of olive oil to the pan.
7. The marinated chicken breasts should be added when the pan is hot. Cook for 5 to 6 minutes on each side or until the chicken is well cooked and the middle is no longer pink. Adjust cooking time for chicken breast thickness.
8. Adding unsalted butter to the pan in the last minutes is optional. For richer flavor, pour melted butter over chicken breasts while cooking.
9. After cooking, take the chicken from the pan and let it rest for a few minutes before cutting or serving.
10. Add fresh parsley before serving to brighten the Luminescent Lemon Pepper Chicken.
11. Serve and Enjoy: Serve this spicy chicken with salad, rice, or roasted vegetables.

NOTE

Changing the amount of zest and juice can alter the strength of the lemon flavor. Fully cooked chicken is 165°F (74°C). This lemon-pepper chicken dish is fragrant and flavorful.

40. ILLUMINATED ICEBERG LETTUCE WRAPS

INGREDIENTS:

For the Filling:

- 1 pound ground chicken or turkey (or tofu for a vegetarian option)
- 2 tablespoons olive oil
- 2 cloves garlic, minced
- 1 small onion, finely chopped
- 1 red bell pepper, diced
- 1 cup mushrooms, finely chopped
- 1 carrot, grated
- 1/4 cup hoisin sauce
- 2 tablespoons soy sauce
- 1 tablespoon rice vinegar
- 1 teaspoon sesame oil
- 1/4 cup chopped green onions
- Salt and pepper to taste
- 1 head iceberg lettuce, leaves separated and cleaned

For Garnish (Optional):

- Sesame seeds
- Chopped cilantro
- Sliced green onions

INSTRUCTIONS:

1. To prepare the filling, place a large skillet or pan over medium-high heat with olive oil. Add the chopped onion, minced garlic, and sauté for two to three minutes or until transparent and aromatic.
2. Cook the Meat or Tofu: Fill the skillet with ground turkey, chicken, or tofu. Break it up and fry using a spatula until it's browned and cooked through.
3. Add the vegetables: Stir in the grated carrot, sliced mushrooms, and diced red bell pepper. Cook the veggies for three to four minutes or until they are soft.
4. In a separate bowl, mix hoisin, soy, rice vinegar, and sesame oil to season the filling. Pour sauce over cooked tofu or chicken and vegetables in pan. Mix thoroughly to combine
5. Add chopped green onions to the pan to finish and season. Cook for one more minute while stirring. If necessary, add more salt and pepper to the seasoning after tasting. Take off the heat.

6. Assemble the Lettuce Wraps: Take individual iceberg leaves, wrap them like tacos or burritos, and then ladle some of the contents into each leaf.
7. Garnish and Serve: You may add chopped cilantro, sesame seeds, and green onions to the filled wraps for flavor and look.
8.
9. Have fun:
10. Present these Luminous Iceberg Lettuce Wraps as a tasty and light appetizer or as a main entrée with extra sides.

NOTE:

> You are welcome to adjust the filling components to your personal preference. You may change the sweetness or saltiness of the sauce and add more veggies. These healthful, adaptable lettuce wraps are ideal for a filling, light supper.

FULL MOON RECIPES:

41. FULL MOON FRUIT TART

INGREDIENTS:

For the Crust:

- 1 1/2 cups all-purpose flour
- 1/2 cup powdered sugar
- 1/4 teaspoon and salt
- 1/2 cup unsalted butter and cold, cut into small cubes
- 1 large egg yolk
- 1-2 tablespoons ice water (if needed)

For the Filling:

- 8 oz cream cheese, softened
- 1/4 cup granulated sugar
- 1 teaspoon vanilla extract
- For the Fruit Topping:
- Assorted fresh fruits (such as strawberries and blueberries, kiwi, raspberries, and grapes) were washed and sliced as needed
- 1/4 cup apricot preserves or jelly for glaze

INSTRUCTIONS:

1. For the crust, grind flour, salt, and powdered sugar until coarse crumbs form. Pulse again with cooled cubed butter.
2. Add water and egg yolk and pulse again when dough comes together. Rehydrate dried dough by adding 1–2 teaspoons of cold water and puls
3. ing until a ball forms.
4. Form a disk of dough and wrap it in plastic. Put it in the fridge for 30 minutes.
5. Turn on oven to 375°F/190°C.
6. Rolled and baked crust.
7. On a lightly floured surface, roll cold dough into a 9-inch tart pan circle. Cover the tart pan's borders and bottom with dough. Cut more dough roughly.

8. Protect the crust from bubbling with parchment paper, aluminum foil, pie weights, or dried beans. Finish baking 18–25 minutes. Remove weights and paper or foil and bake for 5–7 minutes once the crust is golden brown. Allow thorough cooling.
9. Get Filling Ready:
10. The softened cream cheese, granulated sugar, and vanilla essence should be mixed until smooth.
11. Putting the Tart Together:
12. Over the chilled tart shell, evenly distribute the cream cheese filling.
13. Arrange the Fruit: Arrange the sliced fresh fruits on top of the cream cheese mixture in an eye-catching design that mimics the full moon. Use creativity when arranging the fruit!
14. Glaze the Fruit: Microwave the jelly or preserves for a few seconds to thin them down. Lightly drizzle the glaze over the fruits as they are assembled.
15. Chill and Serve: To allow the flavors to mingle, let the Full Moon Fruit Tart sit in the refrigerator for at least one to two hours before serving.
16. Pleasure:
17. This Full Moon Fruit Tart is a lovely treat for any occasion. Just slice and serve.

NOTE:
> Feel free to customize the arrangement of your preferred fresh fruits for the topping according to your taste and inventiveness. This tart serves as a visually attractive dessert centrepiece and is delicious!

42. MOONLIT MISO SOUP

Preparation Time: 15 minutes

Cooking Time: 15 minutes

Total Time: 30 minutes

INGREDIENTS:

- 4 cups dashi (Japanese soup stock)
- 3 tablespoons white miso paste
- 1 cup silken tofu, diced into small cubes
- 1 cup seaweed (wakame), soaked and chopped
- 2 green onions, thinly sliced
- 1 cup shiitake mushrooms, thinly sliced
- 1 tablespoon soy sauce
- 1 tablespoon mirin (optional)
- 1 teaspoon sesame oil
- Chopped chives for garnish
- Cooked rice (optional)

INSTRUCTIONS:

1. Dashi preparation involves heating the dashi in a saucepan until it is warm but not boiling.
2. Add the seaweed, sliced mushrooms, green onions, and diced tofu to the saucepan and vegetables. Once the ingredients are soft, simmer them.
3. To dissolve the miso paste, mix a tiny quantity of boiling broth with the white miso paste in a small dish. Verify that there are no lumps.
4. Miso Paste for Soup: Pour the miso paste mixture into the saucepan. Gradually stir in the miso without bringing the soup to a boil.
5. Soy sauce, sesame oil, and mirin are optional additions to the soup. Adjust the seasoning according to your taste.
6. Optional Rice: For a heartier dinner, serve the cooked rice with the miso soup.
7. Spoon the miso soup into bowls under the moonlight. Sprinkle chopped chives on top for a splash of freshness.

NOTES:
- Savor this comforting miso soup for a nutritious and peaceful experience while it's moonlighting.
- Try several kinds of miso paste to get a variety of tastes.

43. BRIGHTEST BUDDHA BOWL

Preparation Time: 20 minutes

Cooking Time: 15 minutes

Total Time: 35 minutes

INGREDIENTS:

- 1 cup quinoa, cooked
- 1 cup sweet potato, diced
- 1 cup broccoli florets
- 1 cup cherry tomatoes, halved
- 1 cup red cabbage, shredded
- 1 cup cucumber, sliced
- 1 cup carrots, julienned
- 1 avocado, sliced
- 1/2 cup hummus
- 1/4 cup pumpkin seeds (optional)
- Fresh cilantro or parsley for garnish

INSTRUCTIONS:

1. Prepare Quinoa: Cook the quinoa according to the box directions—fluff with a fork and set aside.
2. Broccoli with sweet potatoes roasted:
3. Set oven temperature to 400°F or 200°C.
4. Combine broccoli florets and chopped sweet potatoes with olive oil, salt, and pepper. Roast until soft, about 15 minutes.
5. Put the Bowl Together:
6. Spoon cooked quinoa into each of the serving dishes.
7. On top of the quinoa, divide the roasted sweet potatoes, broccoli, cherry tomatoes, red cabbage, cucumber, carrots, and avocado into parts.
8. Top with Hummus:
9. Put a heaping tablespoon of hummus in the middle of every bowl.
10. Garnish: Add some fresh parsley or cilantro and, if desired, sprinkle in some pumpkin seeds.
11. Dressing (Optional): Drizzle with your preferred dressing or a straightforward vinaigrette.

12. Serve: Toss the ingredients together just before eating for a tasty mixture, and serve immediately.

NOTES:
- ➢ Add your preferred grains, meats, or veggies to your bowl.
- ➢ Try a variety of hummus tastes to offer even more variation.

44. LUNAR ECLIPSE LAVA CAKE

Preparation Time: 15 minutes

Baking Time: 12 minutes

Total Time: 27 minutes

INGREDIENTS:

- 1/2 cup (1 stick) unsalted butter
- 1 cup dark chocolate chips or chunks
- 2 large eggs
- 2 large egg yolks
- 1/3 cup granulated sugar
- 1 teaspoon vanilla extract
- 1/4 cup all-purpose flour
- 1/4 teaspoon salt
- 1/2 teaspoon instant coffee powder (optional, enhances chocolate flavor)
- Powdered sugar for dusting (optional)
- Vanilla ice cream for serving (optional)

INSTRUCTIONS:

1. Turn on the Oven: Set the temperature to 425°F (220°C). Flour and grease four ramekins or tiny baking dishes.
2. Melt Chocolate and Butter: In a bowl that is safe to use in the microwave, melt the dark chocolate and butter together for 20 seconds at a time, stirring in between each interval until the mixture is smooth. Alternatively, melt using a double boiler.
3. Mix the eggs, egg yolks, and granulated sugar in a separate basin until thoroughly blended to prepare the batter.
4. Stir in the melted butter and chocolate. Add vanilla extract thoroughly.
5. Mix in salt and all-purpose flour. If using instant coffee powder, add it now. Just fold the dry and wet ingredients together.
6. Fill Ramekins: Distribute batter evenly among prepared
7. ramekins.
8. For 12 minutes, or until the center is soft and the edges are firm, bake the ramekins on a baking sheet. Get the oven

ready.

9. Let the cakes cool for a minute before serving. Flip each lava cake onto a dish after knife-loosening the edges.
10. Vanilla ice cream and powdered sugar are optional toppings.

NOTES:
- Vary the baking time according to the desired consistency of the lava and your oven.
- Try a variety of chocolate varieties to get a wide range of tastes.

45. ILLUMINATING ICE CREAM SANDWICHES

Preparation Time: 20 minutes

Freezing Time: 2 hours

Total Time: 2 hours 20 minutes

INGREDIENTS:
- 1 cup all-purpose flour
- 1/2 cup unsweetened cocoa powder
- 1/2 teaspoon baking soda
- 1/4 teaspoon salt
- 1/2 cup unsalted butter, softened
- 3/4 cup granulated sugar
- 1 large egg
- 1 teaspoon vanilla extract
- Your favorite ice cream flavor (e.g., vanilla, chocolate, strawberry)
- Sprinkles or edible glitter for decoration

INSTRUCTIONS:
1. Fire up the oven: Preheat the oven to 350°F (175°C). Line a baking sheet with parchment paper.
2. Prepare cookie dough:
3. Sift flour, baking soda, cocoa powder, and salt in a medium bowl. Set aside.
4. Whip melted butter and granulated sugar in a separate dish until fluffy.
5. Blend egg and Vanilla until smooth.
6. Mix until a soft dough forms, then add dry ingredients slowly.
7. Form and Bake: Split the dough. Roll each portion into a 1.5-inch log.
8. After wrapping in plastic, refrigerate the logs for one hour.
9. After preparing the baking sheet, cut the logs into 1/4-inch circles.
10. Bake until edges are crisp, 10–12 minutes. Allow cookies to cool completely.
11. After freezing, add a scoop of your favorite ice cream on one cookie's flat side to make Ice Cream
12. Sandwiches.
13. Lay a cookie flat-side down
14. on ice cream and press.
15. Roll ice cream sandwich edges in sprinkles or glitter to celebrate.

16. Freeze ice cream sandwiches for 1–2 hours until solid.
17. Let your enlightened ice cream sandwiches
18. settle from the freezer before serving!

NOTES:

Try experimenting with other cookie tastes to go well with the ice cream.

Use edible glitter or various sprinkled colors to create an eye-catching effect.

46. FULL MOON FETTUCCINE ALFREDO

Preparation Time: 15 minutes

Cooking Time: 15 minutes

Total Time: 30 minutes

INGREDIENTS:

- 1 pound fettuccine pasta
- 1/2 cup unsalted butter
- 1 cup heavy cream
- 1 cup grated Parmesan cheese
- Salt and black pepper to taste
- 1/2 teaspoon garlic powder (optional)
- Fresh parsley, chopped, for garnish
- Additional Parmesan for serving

INSTRUCTIONS:

1. Follow the box instructions to boil fettuccine in a large saucepan of salted water. Set aside after draining.
2. For Alfredo
3. sauce, melt butter in a big pan on medium. Simmer heavy cream a
4. fter melting.
5. Add cheddar, cream the sauce, lower the heat to low, and stir in grated Parmesan cheese.
6. Season Alfredo sauce with salt, black pepper, and garlic powder. Adjust spice to taste.
7. Mix with pasta: Combine cooked fettuccine and Alfredo sauce in a pan. To coat pasta evenly with sauce, toss.
8. To serve, arrange the Full Moon Fettuccine Alfredo on a platter and sprinkle with parsley. If desired, add more Parmesan cheese on top.
9. Celestial Presentation (Optional): Arrange the pasta on the dish in a circular form to resemble a full moon.

NOTES:

- Before adding the cream, try sautéing chopped garlic in the butter for more flavor.
- Use freshly grated Parmesan for the most texture and taste.

47. CELESTIAL CHARCUTERIE BOARD

Preparation Time: 30 minutes

Assembly Time: 15 minutes

Total Time: 45 minutes

INGREDIENTS:

Cheeses:

- Brie or Camembert (moon-shaped if available)
- Blue cheese (for a starry effect)
- Aged cheddar or gouda

Meats:

- Prosciutto or other cured meats folded into star shapes
- Salami or pepperoni slices

Fruits:

- Grapes or berries
- Figs or dates
- Sliced apples or pears
- Crackers and Breads:
- Assorted crackers
- Baguette slices or breadsticks
- Nuts and Dried Fruits:
- Almonds, walnuts, or cashews
- Dried apricots or figs
- Spreads and Sauces:
- Honey or fig jam (for drizzling)
- Whole grain mustard or Dijon
- Fruit preserves
- Extras:
- Dark chocolate squares or truffles (constellation shapes if available)
- Edible flowers for decoration

INSTRUCTIONS:

1. Cut the cheeses into slices and place them on the board. If using Brie or Camembert, cut them into moon shapes.
2. Prosciutto or other cured meats can be folded into the shape of stars.
3. Spreads such as mustard, honey, and preserves should be placed in little dishes on the board.
4. Bring the Board Together:
5. Start arranging the cheeses on the board in different places.
6. Using a design like a constellation, arrange the cured meats.
7. Place berry or grape bunches in the spaces to create the illusion of a galaxy.
8. Arrange the dried fruits, nuts, and cut fruits on the board.
9. Add Bread and Crackers: Arrange the bread and crackers on the board in different locations to create a variety of textures.
10. Drizzle and Decorate: Drizzle honey over the cheeses and meats to add something extra.
11. For a heavenly and eye-catching arrangement, add edible flowers.
12. Confections and Extras: Arrange pieces or truffles made of dark chocolate in a strategic pattern on the board.
13. Think of incorporating tiny constellation patterns with edible silver or gold dust.
14. To serve, place the Celestial Charcuterie Board at the center of your table and start having fun!

NOTES:

➢ Use your imagination when arranging, trying to go for a heavenly and starry motif.
➢ To improve the presentation overall, use unusual or themed serving utensils.

48. RADIANT RAMEN NOODLES

Preparation Time: 15 minutes

Cooking Time: 15 minutes

Total Time: 30 minutes

INGREDIENTS:

For the Broth:

- 4 cups chicken or vegetable broth
- 2 cloves garlic, minced
- 1 tablespoon ginger, grated
- 2 tablespoons soy sauce
- 1 tablespoon miso paste
- 1 tablespoon sesame oil
- Salt and pepper to taste

For the Noodles and Toppings:

- 2 packs of ramen noodles (discard the seasoning packets)
- 1 cup carrots, julienned or grated
- 1 cup red cabbage, thinly sliced
- 1 cup baby spinach or kale leaves
- 1 cup bell peppers, thinly sliced (assorted colors)
- 1 cup shiitake or button mushrooms, sliced
- 4 boiled eggs, halved
- Green onion slices with sesame seeds for garnish
- Lime wedges for serving

INSTRUCTIONS:

1. Prepare broth by heating sesame oil in a pot on medium. Add grated ginger and minced garlic and simmer for 1 minute.
2. Add the miso paste, soy sauce, and broth. Bring to a simmer and cook for ten minutes. Season with salt and pepper to taste.
3. Cook Noodles: Prepare the ramen noodles per the directions on the package. After draining, set away.

4. Prepare the Vegetables: Saute the bell peppers, mushrooms, red cabbage, and carrots in a separate pan until they are soft but have retained their color.
5. Assemble Bowls: Spoon-cooked noodles are arranged into individual bowls.
6. Over the noodles, ladle the heated broth.
7. Add the veggies and Toppings: Place the cooked eggs, spinach, or kale, and sautéed veggies over the noodles.
8. Garnish: Top the dishes with chopped green onions and sesame seeds.
9. Present: Present the Radiant Ramen Noodles alongside slices of lime.

NOTES:
- Tailor the vegetable choices to your tastes and the produce in season.
- If desired, add more sriracha or chili oil to adjust the spiciness.

49. LUNAR LASAGNA ROLL-UPS

Preparation Time: 30 minutes

Baking Time: 25 minutes

Total Time: 55 minutes

INGREDIENTS:

For the Filling:

- 8 noodles for lasagna, cooked to package directions
- 1 pound ground beef or Italian sausage
- 1 onion, finely chopped
- 3 cloves garlic, minced
- 1 can (14 oz) crushed tomatoes
- 1 can (6 oz) tomato paste
- 1 teaspoon dried oregano
- 1 teaspoon dried basil
- Salt and pepper to taste
- 1 cup ricotta cheese
- 1 cup shredded mozzarella cheese
- 1/2 cup grated Parmesan cheese
- Fresh basil or parsley for garnish

For the Presentation:

- Mozzarella slices or shapes for the moon phases (crescent, half, full)
- Additional grated Parmesan for a stardust effect

INSTRUCTIONS:

1. Prepare the Lasagna Noodles: Follow the directions on the package to prepare the lasagna noodles. Drain and set aside.
2. Get the filling ready:
3. Pan-brown Italian sausage or ground beef over medium heat. Soften minced garlic and onions.
4. Stir in
5. salt, pepper, dried oregano, basil, smashed tomatoes, and tomato paste. Ten to fifteen minutes, simmer.

6. Use a basin to combine ricotta, mozzarella, and Parmesan.
7. Lay down the cooked lasagna noodles on a flat surface to assemble the roll-ups. Top each noodle with a layer of the cheese mixture and a layer of the meat sauce.
8. Roll and Place: After rolling each lasagna noodle, put it on a baking dish with the seam facing down.
9. Make Moon Phases: Place shapes or slices of mozzarella on top of the roll-ups to make lunar phases. Moon phases that are full, crescent, and half can all be used.
10. In a preheated 375°F oven, melt and bubble cheese for 20–25 minutes.
11. Garnish: To create the appearance of stardust, sprinkle some more grated Parmesan over the dish. Add some parsley or basil for a garnish.
12. Present: Present the Lunar Lasagna Roll-Ups with an astronomical touch!

NOTES:
- Use cookie cutters or carefully cut the mozzarella slices to create unique moon phase designs.
- To make the filling to your taste, adjust the ingredients.

50. MIDNIGHT MOON PIES

Preparation Time: 30 minutes

Chilling Time: 1 hour

Total Time: 1 hour 30 minutes

INGREDIENTS:

For the Cookies:

- 1 cup all-purpose flour
- 1/2 cup unsweetened cocoa powder
- 1/2 teaspoon baking soda
- 1/4 teaspoon baking powder
- 1/4 teaspoon salt
- 1/2 cup unsalted butter, softened
- 3/4 cup granulated sugar
- 1 large egg
- 1 teaspoon vanilla extract

For the Marshmallow Filling:

- 1 cup marshmallow fluff or marshmallow creme
- 1/2 cup powdered sugar
- For the Chocolate Coating:
- 8 oz dark chocolate, chopped
- 2 tablespoons coconut oil

INSTRUCTIONS:

1. Get the cookies ready:
2. Mix flour, baking powder, soda, cocoa powder, and salt in a bowl. Set aside.
3. Beat butter and powdered sugar in a separate bowl until foamy.
4. Add egg and vanilla essence and stir well.
5. Mix until a soft dough forms, then gently add dry ingredients.
6. Wrap dough in plastic
7. and
8. chill 30 minutes.
9. Slice and roll:

10. Circle cookie cutters. After baking sheet prep, place rounds.
11. Bake until edges are crisp, 10–12 minutes. Allow cookies to cool completely.
12. To make the marshmallow filling, place marshmallow crème or fluff in a dish and whisk in powdered sugar until smooth.
13. To assemble the Moon Pies, spread a layer of marshmallow filling on half of the cookies' flat sides.
14. To resemble sandwiches, place the remaining cookies on top.
15. Chill: Put the completed moon pies in the fridge for at least half an hour
16. to set.
17. Chocolate Coating is made by melting coconut oil and dark chocolate in a heatproof bowl over a double boiler or microwave.
18. Coat Moon Pies: D Dip each cooled moon pie in melted chocolate to cover evenly.
19. After transferring the coated moon pies to a tray lined with paper, refrigerate for a further half hour.
20. Serve: Savor your Midnight Moon Pies with your preferred warm beverage or hot cocoa!

NOTES:
- For more variation, try out various cookie sizes and shapes.
- For a midnight sparkle, top with crumbled dark chocolate or edible glitter.

WANING GIBBOUS RECIPES:

51. WANING WALNUT WAFFLES

Preparation Time: 15 minutes

Cooking Time: 15 minutes

Total Time: 30 minutes

INGREDIENTS:

- 2 cups all-purpose flour
- 2 tablespoons sugar
- 1 tablespoon baking powder
- 1/2 teaspoon salt
- 1 3/4 cups milk
- 1/3 cup vegetable oil
- 2 large eggs
- 1 teaspoon vanilla extract
- 1/2 cup chopped walnuts
- Maple syrup for serving
- Fresh berries for garnish

INSTRUCTIONS:

1. Waffle Iron Preparation: Follow the manufacturer's recommendations for waffle iron preheating.
2. A big basin is the best place to mix the sugar, baking powder, and salt.
3. Stir together the dry ingredients. Wet Vanilla, vegetable oil, milk, and eggs should be added to a separate bowl.
4. Stir to blend the wet and dry ingredients slightly. Add the wet components to the dry ingredients. Take care not to overmix; some lumps are OK.
5. Include Walnuts:
6. Add the chopped walnuts to the waffle batter and gently mix them in.
7. To make waffles, lightly sprinkle nonstick cooking spray on the waffle iron.
8. After preheating the waffle iron, pour the batter over it in the recommended amount and cook it as directed by the maker until the waffles are crisp and golden brown.

9. Present: Accompany the Waning Walnut Waffles with fresh fruit and maple syrup.

NOTE:
- Consider incorporating nutmeg or cinnamon into the batter for extra taste.
- The walnuts' nutty taste is enhanced when toasted before being included in the batter.

52. GLOW-OUT GRANOLA PARFAIT

Preparation Time: 15 minutes

Assembly Time: 5 minutes

Total Time: 20 minutes

INGREDIENTS:

For the Granola:

- 2 cups rolled oats
- 1/2 cup chopped nuts
- 1/4 cup honey or maple syrup
- 2 tablespoons coconut oil, melted
- 1 teaspoon vanilla extract
- A pinch of salt

For the Parfait:

- 2 cups Greek yogurt or yogurt of your choice
- 1 cup mixed berries (strawberries, blueberries, raspberries)
- 1/2 cup mango, diced
- 1/4 cup chia seeds
- 2 tablespoons honey or agave nectar
- Edible glitter or colorful sprinkles for a "glow-out" effect

INSTRUCTIONS:

1. Get the granola ready:
2. Before placing the dish in the oven, heat it to 325°F (163°C).
3. With the chopped nuts, honey/maple syrup, vanilla essence, and a bit of salt added to the melted coconut oil, swirl to combine. Finally, mix in the rolled oats.
4. Distribute the batter onto a baking sheet that has been lined with parchment paper.
5. After 15–20 minutes of baking, toss occasionally to prevent sticking. Bake until golden brown. Allow enough time for it to cool.
6. In individual serving plates or glasses, layer the parfait ingredients: Greek yogurt, diced mango, mixed berries, and a sprinkle of granola.
7. To assemble the parfait, arrange Greek yogurt, chopped mango, mixed berries, and a dollop of granola in serving dishes or glasses.

8. Continue layering until you get to the top.
9. After scattering chia seeds, add a little sweetness by drizzling honey or agave nectar over the top layer.
10. Glow-out Effect: To create a "glow-out" effect, top with edible glitter or vibrant sprinkles.
11. Serve: Present the Glow-out Granola Parfait immediately, and savor its colorful and delectable layers!

NOTE:
- Personalize the parfait by adding your preferred nuts and fruits.
- Select a range of vibrant berries to create a visually striking arrangement.

53. SUBSIDING SPINACH SALAD

Preparation Time: 15 minutes

Total Time: 15 minutes

INGREDIENTS:

For the Salad:

- 6 cups fresh baby spinach and washed and dried
- 1 cup cherry tomatoes, halved
- 1 cucumber, sliced
- 1/2 red onion, thinly sliced
- 1 cup crumbled feta cheese
- 1/2 cup black olives, pitted
- 1/4 cup pine nuts, toasted

For the Dressing:

- 1/4 cup extra-virgin olive oil
- 2 tablespoons balsamic vinegar
- 1 teaspoon Dijon mustard
- 1 clove garlic, minced
- Salt and black pepper to taste

INSTRUCTIONS:

1. Prepare the salad ingredients by combining cucumber slices, thinly sliced red onion, black olives, crumbled feta cheese, and toasted pine nuts with fresh baby spinach in a large salad dish.
2. Garlic, salt, pepper, balsamic vinegar, Dijon mustard, and extra virgin olive oil are the dressing components. Combine all of them in a small bowl. Add the seasoning that suits your taste.
3. Drizzle the salad ingredients with the dressing before tossing to serve.
4. Lightly mix the salad so all of the ingredients are coated with the dressing.
5. Refrigerate (Optional): To allow the flavors to mingle, refrigerate the salad for fifteen to thirty minutes.
6. Serve the Subsiding Spinach Salad family-style or by dividing it among separate dishes.
7. As a garnish, add more feta cheese and pine nuts.

NOTES:
- For more protein, add grilled chicken, shrimp, or chickpeas.
- Feel free to add more toppings or your preferred veggies to personalize the salad.

54. LUNAR LEMON POPPY SEED MUFFINS

> Preparation Time: 15 minutes
> Baking Time: 18-20 minutes
> Total Time: 35 minutes

INGREDIENTS:

- 2 cups all-purpose flour
- 1 cup granulated sugar
- 1 tablespoon poppy seeds
- 1 tablespoon lemon zest
- 1 teaspoon baking powder
- 1/2 teaspoon baking soda
- 1/4 teaspoon salt
- 1/2 cup unsalted butter, melted
- 3/4 cup buttermilk
- 2 large eggs
- 1/4 cup fresh lemon juice
- 1 teaspoon vanilla extract

For the Glaze:

- 1 cup powdered sugar
- 2 tablespoons fresh lemon juice
- Lemon zest for garnish (optional)

INSTRUCTIONS:

1. Place the rack in the oven: Bring the oven temperature up to 190 degrees Celsius, or 375 degrees Fahrenheit. Use paper liners or butter the muffin pan cups to get them ready.
2. Combine the dry ingredients:
3. Gather all of the ingredients in a large basin: poppy seeds, sugar, lemon zest, baking soda, baking powder, salt, and flour.
4. Mix Wet Ingredients: In a separate dish, mix the eggs, buttermilk, vanilla essence, lemon juice, and melted butter.
5. Integrate the Dry and Wet Mixtures:
6. Combine the wet and dry components by pouring them together. Mix until barely incorporated. It's all right to have some lumps; don't overmix.

7. Fill Muffin Cups: Using a spoon, measure the batter and fill each to approximately two-thirds of the way.
8. Poke a toothpick into the center and remove it clean; this should take around 18 to 20 minutes in a preheated oven. Very nice.
9. While the muffins are in the oven, mix up the glaze ingredients. Toss the powdered sugar and lemon juice in a small bowl to combine.
10. Once the muffins have cooled slightly after taking them out of the oven, brush the tops with the muffin glaze.
11. Optional garnish: You can top it off with more lemon zest if you like.
12. The Lunar Lemon Poppy Seed Muffins should sit for a few minutes in the muffin pan before transferring to a wire rack to cool completely before being served.

NOTES:
- Consider incorporating more lemon zest into the batter for an additional flavor explosion.
- Add extra powdered sugar or lemon juice to adjust the glaze's consistency if necessary.

55. DIMINISHING DARK CHOCOLATE TRUFFLES

Preparation Time: 30 minutes

Chilling Time: 2 hours

Total Time: 2 hours 30 minutes

INGREDIENTS:

- 8 ounces (about 227g) high-quality dark chocolate, finely chopped
- 1/2 cup (120ml) heavy cream
- 2 tablespoons unsalted butter
- 1 teaspoon pure vanilla extract
- For coating, you can use cocoa powder, powdered sugar, or minced nuts.

INSTRUCTIONS:

1. Finely chop the dark chocolate, then transfer it to a heatproof dish. The cake should be completely cooled on a wire rack after 10 minutes of baking.
2. If you are around anything that may be used to boil water, stay away from it.
3. Over the coarsely chopped chocolate, pour the warmed cream and butter combination. Do not touch it for at least two minutes.
4. Melt and smooth out the chocolate by whisking the mixture gently once it has set.
5. Mix in the vanilla essence with a whisk until well incorporated.
6. Chill: Cover the bowl and refrigerate it for at least two hours, or until the mixture becomes manageable.
7. Shape the truffles: After the chocolate mixture has cooled, scoop out tiny bits with a spoon or melon baller.
8. With your palms, roll each part into a ball. As they warm up, you may notice a tiny decrease in their size.
9. Coat with Sugar or Cocoa Powder: To coat the truffles, roll them in sugar, cocoa powder, or finely chopped nuts.
10. Chill Again (Optional): If the truffles have softened throughout the shaping procedure, refrigerate them for a further 15 to 30 minutes.
11. Serve the Diminishing Dark Chocolate Truffles by arranging them on a serving platter and dig in!

NOTES:
- You may enhance the flavor of the chocolate mixture by adding a tablespoon of your preferred liqueur, such as coffee or Grand Marnier.
- Tailor the coatings to your desired look and feel.

56. FADING FIG FLATBREAD

Preparation Time: 15 minutes

Cooking Time: 15 minutes

Total Time: 30 minutes

INGREDIENTS:

For the Flatbread:

- 1 store-bought pizza dough or flatbread
- 2 tablespoons olive oil
- 1 clove garlic, minced
- 1/2 teaspoon dried thyme
- Salt and black pepper to taste

For the Toppings:

- 6-8 fresh figs, sliced
- 1/2 cup crumbled goat cheese
- 1/4 cup caramelized onions
- 2 tablespoons balsamic reduction
- Fresh arugula for garnish

INSTRUCTIONS:

1. Preheat Oven: Follow the pizza dough or flatbread packaging directions to preheat your oven.
2. To prepare the flatbread, roll out the pizza dough or flatbread to the required thickness on a surface dusted with flour.
3. Season with olive oil, minced garlic, dried thyme, salt, and black pepper in a small bowl to bake. Drizzle the flatbread with this mixture.
4. After putting the flatbread on a pizza stone or baking sheet, bake it in the preheated oven until it is cooked through and golden brown.
5. Put Together the Toppings:
6. After the flatbread bakes, evenly top with sliced figs, caramelized onions, and crumbled goat cheese.

7. Drizzle Balsamic Reduction: Drizzle balsamic reduction over the figs and cheese to enhance the richness and flavor depth.
8. Finish with Arugula: Add some fresh arugula to the Fading Fig Flatbread to make it spicy, colorful pop.
9. Cut and Present: Cut the flatbread into individual servings and present them right away.

NOTES:
- Onions may be made into caramelized onions by slicing them thinly and cooking them in olive oil over medium-low heat until they become a golden brown and become sweet.
- For an extra kick, top with some crushed red pepper flakes

57. CRESCENT CARROT CAKE

Preparation Time: 20 minutes

Baking Time: 25-30 minutes

Cooling Time: 1 hour

Total Time: 1 hour 50 minutes

INGREDIENTS:

For the Carrot Cake:

- 2 cups grated carrots
- 1 1/2 cups all-purpose flour
- 1 cup granulated sugar
- 1/2 cup brown sugar, packed
- 1/2 cup vegetable oil
- 3 large eggs
- 1 teaspoon vanilla extract
- 1 teaspoon ground cinnamon
- 1/2 teaspoon ground nutmeg
- 1/2 teaspoon ground ginger
- 1/2 teaspoon baking powder
- 1/2 teaspoon baking soda
- 1/4 teaspoon salt
- 1/2 cup crushed pineapple, drained
- 1/2 cup chopped walnuts or pecans

For the Cream Cheese Frosting:

- 8 oz cream cheese, softened
- 1/2 cup unsalted butter, softened
- 4 cups powdered sugar
- 1 teaspoon vanilla extract

INSTRUCTIONS:

1. Fahrenheit (or 175 degrees Celsius) is the heat setting for an oven. Preheat a cake pan, either a circular one with a crescent shape or a regular round one, and dust it with flour.
2. Whisk together the carrot cake batter.
3. Grated carrots, flour, brown sugar, granulated sugar, oil from vegetables, eggs, vanilla essence, ground nutmeg, ground ginger, ground cinnamon, baking soda, etc. should all be mixed together in a substantial basin. Beat on high speed until smooth and velvety.
4. Toss in the crushed pineapple and chopped nuts if using.
5. Before placing the batter in the cake pan, make sure to level the top.
6. After
7. 25 to 30 minutes in a preheated oven, poke a toothpick into the middle and it should come out clean.
8. After 10 minutes, take
9. the cake out of the pan and let it cool completely on a wire rack.Blended cheese, melted butter
10. Melted butter, cream cheese, powdered sugar, and vanilla extract
11. are whisked together to make cream cheese frosting.
12. As soon as the cake has cooled, spread the cream cheese frosting over it. You have the option to utilize a crescent shape for both the top and the entire cake when frosting. The choice is yours.
13. More chopped almonds, shredded carrots, or a sprinkle of cinnamon will make a lovely topping for this Crescent Carrot Cake.
14. Slice the cake and serve it after it has cooled to room temperature. You owe it to yourself, Crescent, to give carrot cake a go. Enjoy yourselves!

NOTES:

- Change the powdered sugar in the cream cheese frosting to get the right sweetness.
- Add coconut or raisins to add more texture to the carrot cake batter.

58. DWINDLING DAHL SOUP

Preparation Time: 15 minutes

Cooking Time: 40 minutes

Total Time: 55 minutes

INGREDIENTS:

- 1 cup red lentils, washed and drained
- 1 large onion, finely chopped
- 3 cloves garlic, minced
- 1 tablespoon ginger, grated
- 1 tablespoon vegetable oil
- 1 teaspoon cumin seeds
- 1 teaspoon ground turmeric
- 1 teaspoon ground coriander
- 1/2 teaspoon chili powder (adjust to taste)
- 1 can (14 oz) diced tomatoes
- 4 cups vegetable broth
- 1 can (14 oz) coconut milk
- Salt and black pepper to taste
- Fresh cilantro, chopped, for garnish
- Lemon wedges for serving

INSTRUCTIONS:

1. Rinse Lentils: Until the water runs clear, rinse the red lentils under cold water.
2. To sauté aromatics, place a large saucepan over medium heat with vegetable oil. Sprinkle in the cumin seeds and watch them pop.
3. Add the grated ginger, minced garlic, and chopped onions. The onions should be sautéed until transparent.
4. Add Spices: Add chili powder, ground coriander, and ground turmeric. To thoroughly mix the spices with the aromatics, stir well.
5. Cook Lentils: Place the rinsed red lentils in the saucepan and toss them with the aromatics and spices.
6. Pour in the chopped tomatoes (together with their juices) and the veggie broth. Heat the mixture until it boils.

7. Simmer: After lowering the heat, cover the pot and let it there for approximately half an hour, or until the flavors have melded and the lentils are tender.
8. After you've mixed everything thoroughly, add the coconut milk. Add another ten to fifteen minutes
9. of simmering time.
10. To taste, season the dwindling Dahl
11. soup with salt and black pepper.
12. Spoon the soup into individual bowls and top with garnishes. For presentation, top with chopped cilantro and serve with lemon wedges.

NOTES:
- You may use more or less chili powder to change the spiciness.
- For a full dinner, serve the soup with naan bread or over rice.

59. VANISHING VEGGIE STIR-FRY

Preparation Time: 15 minutes

Cooking Time: 10 minutes

Total Time: 25 minutes

INGREDIENTS:

For the Stir-Fry:

- 2 cups broccoli florets
- 1 cup sliced carrots
- 1 bell pepper, thinly sliced (any color)
- 1 cup snap peas, ends trimmed
- 1 cup sliced mushrooms
- 1 cup tofu or chicken, cubed (optional)
- 2 tablespoons vegetable oil

For the Sauce:

- 1/4 cup soy sauce
- 2 tablespoons oyster sauce
- 1 tablespoon hoisin sauce
- 1 tablespoon rice vinegar
- 1 tablespoon sesame oil
- 1 tablespoon cornstarch
- 2 teaspoons sugar
- 1 teaspoon minced garlic
- 1 teaspoon minced ginger
- Red pepper flakes or Sriracha for heat (optional)

For Serving:

- Cooked rice or noodles

INSTRUCTIONS:

1. To whip up the sauce, take a small bowl and mix together hoisin sauce, soy sauce, oyster sauce, cornstarch, sugar, rice vinegar, minced ginger, and sesame oil. Take it off the tabletop.
2. Sauté Tofu or Chicken (Optional): In a wok or big pan, sauté the tofu or chicken with a small amount of vegetable oil until browned. Take out of the pan and place aside.
3. Stir-Fry Vegetables: Add two teaspoons of vegetable oil to the same pan. Add the bell pepper, snap peas, broccoli, carrots, and mushrooms, and stir-fry until they are crisp-tender.
4. Mix Sauce: Add cooked chicken or tofu back to the pan (if using). Cover the protein and veggies with the sauce. Mix everything.
5. Cook Until Sauce Thickens: Cook the veggies and protein for two to three minutes or until the sauce thickens and coats them.
6. Taste and adjust the seasoning, adding Sriracha or red pepper flakes for more heat if preferred.
7. Serve: Present the Disappearing Vegetable Stir-fry over noodles or cooked rice.

NOTES:

- Feel free to alter the veggies to suit your tastes or what you have on hand.
- You may also use shrimp or meat for extra protein.

60. WANING WALNUT BROWNIES

Preparation Time: 15 minutes

Baking Time: 25-30 minutes

Cooling Time: 1 hour

Total Time: 1 hour 45 minutes

INGREDIENTS:

- 1 cup (2 sticks) unsalted butter, melted
- 2 cups granulated sugar
- 4 large eggs
- 1 teaspoon vanilla extract
- 1 cup all-purpose flour
- 1/2 cup unsweetened cocoa powder
- 1/4 teaspoon salt
- 1 cup chopped walnuts
- Powdered sugar for dusting (optional)

INSTRUCTIONS:

1. The cake should be taken out of the pan and allowed to cool completely on a wire rack after 10 minutes.
2. Combine Wet Ingredients: Thoroughly whisk together melted butter and powdered sugar using a large mixing basin.
3. Add the Vanilla and Eggs. Whisk well after each egg addition, one at a time. Add the vanilla essence and stir.
4. Mix Dry Ingredients: Sieve flour, cocoa powder, and salt in a separate bowl.
5. Add the Dry Ingredients: Stir the dry ingredients into the wet components until they are incorporated. Add the dry ingredients gradually. Avoid over-mixing.
6. Add Walnuts: Stir in the finely chopped walnuts, setting aside a few for the garnish.
7. Before baking, make sure the batter is spread out evenly in the pan. Toss in the walnuts that you set aside.
8. It should take 25 to 30 minutes in a preheated oven, or until batter rather than wet crumbs comes out, before you may put a toothpick in the center.

9. After baking, transfer the brownie pan to a wire rack to cool completely.
10. Cut and Dust (Optional): After the brownies cool, cut them into square pieces. If desired, dust with powdered sugar.
11. Present: Present the Waning Walnut Brownies and savor them!

NOTES:

- If you want an extra dose of decadence, throw in some chocolate chips with the batter.
- Don't overbake; brownies that are just barely done are fudgier.

LAST QUARTER RECIPES:

61. LAST QUARTER QUICHE

Preparation Time: 30 minutes

Baking Time: 40-45 minutes

Total Time: 1 hour 15 minutes

INGREDIENTS:

For the Quiche Filling:

- 1 pre-made pie crust (store-bought or homemade)
- 1 cup cooked and diced ham or bacon
- 1 cup shredded Swiss or Gruyere cheese
- bell peppers, chopped (any color)

, half a cup

- Red onion, chopped, 1/2 cup
- 1/2 cup chopped spinach or kale, sautéed and drained
- 4 large eggs
- 1 cup whole milk or half-and-half
- Salt and black pepper to taste
- A pinch of nutmeg (optional)

For the Crust (if homemade):

- 1 1/4 cups all-purpose flour
- 1/2 cup cold unsalted butter, diced
- 1/4 teaspoon salt
- 2-3 tablespoons ice water

INSTRUCTIONS:

1. Oven Prep: Set the oven's temperature to 375°F, or 190°C.
2. Ready the Crust, if it's homemade:
3. Put the flour, salt, and chilled cubed butter in a food processor. Pulse until coarse crumbs form from the mixture.
4. Add the ice water, and pulse one spoonful until the dough comes together.
5. After shaping the dough into a disk, cover it with plastic and set it aside to cool for half an hour.
6. Roll out the chilled dough and transfer it to a pie plate using a floured surface.
7. Optional Pre-Bake Crust: Preheat the oven to 375°F and bake the Crust for 8 to 10 minutes, or until it is just set. Although optional, this step helps avoid a soggy crust.
8. Mix the eggs, milk or half-and-half, nutmeg (if using), salt, and black pepper in a bowl to make the quiche filling.
9. Ingredients to layer: Arrange bell peppers, red onion, shredded cheese, sautéed spinach or kale, and ham or bacon in layers within the pie shell.
10. Pour Egg Mixture: Evenly distribute the egg mixture over the stacked components.
11. Bake: Bake the Last Quarter Quiche for 40 to 45 minutes, or until the top is browned and the middle is set.
12. Chill and Present: Allow the quiche to chill for a few minutes before slicing. Heat or serve at room temperature.

NOTES:

- Feel free to personalize the quiche with your preferred cheeses, veggies, or meats.
- If using a store-bought crust, bake it according to the prebaking directions on the package.

62. LUNAR LOX BAGEL SANDWICHES

Preparation Time: 15 minutes

Total Time: 15 minutes

INGREDIENTS:

- 4 bagels (your choice of flavor), sliced and toasted
- 8 oz smoked salmon (lox)
- 1/2 cup cream cheese, softened
- 1 tablespoon capers
- 1/4 red onion, thinly sliced
- 1 medium tomato, sliced
- Fresh dill sprigs for garnish
- Lemon wedges for serving

INSTRUCTIONS:

1. To prepare the bagels, slice, and toast until they reach the appropriate crispness.
2. Spread Cream Cheese: Evenly cover both halves of each bagel with a thick coating of softened cream cheese.
3. Layer Smoked Salmon: Spread a heaping helping of lox (smoked salmon) on the underside of each bagel.
4. Include toppings:
5. Drizzle the salmon with capers, sprinkle with tomato slices, and finely slice the red onion.
6. Garnish: Add some fresh dill sprigs to the Lunar Lox Bagel Sandwiches.
7. Present the bagel sandwiches with lemon wedges so guests can squeeze them over the lox.

NOTES:

- Add other toppings, such as avocado or cucumber slices, to personalize the sandwich.
- Pick your preferred bagel kind, whether sesame, plain, everything, or a custom taste.

63. FADING FRUIT SMOOTHIE BOWL

Preparation Time: 10 minutes

Total Time: 10 minutes

INGREDIENTS:

For the Smoothie Base:

- 1 frozen banana
- 1 cup mixed berries
- 1/2 cup mango chunks (fresh or frozen)
- 1/2 cup plain Greek yogurt
- Almond milk, or your choice of milk, 1/2 cup
- One spoonful of maple syrup or honey

For Toppings:

- Sliced kiwi
- Sliced strawberries
- Blueberries
- Granola
- Chia seeds
- Shredded coconut
- Edible flowers (optional)

INSTRUCTIONS:

1. Prepare the smoothie base by combining the frozen banana, Greek yogurt, almond milk, mango chunks, mixed berries, and honey or maple syrup (if used) in a blender.
2. Blend till creamy and smooth. If additional liquid is required to reach the right consistency, add it.
3. Transfer to a bowl:
4. Transfer the blended drink to a bowl.
5. Arrange Toppings: On the surface of the smoothie, arrange the sliced kiwi, strawberries, blueberries, granola, chia seeds, shredded coconut, and any other toppings you would like.
6. Arrange the toppings in a way that produces a fading effect from one side of the dish to the other. For instance, begin with a single fruit concentrate and then work your way out to include more fruits and toppings.

7. Add Edible Flowers (Optional): Garnish with edible flowers to create a visually appealing and vibrant appearance.
8. Serve Right Away: Savor the Fading Fruit Smoothie Bowl as soon as possible to enjoy its brilliant, fresh flavor.

NOTES:
- Depending on your tastes and what's in season, try a variety of fruits and toppings.
- Protein powder or nut butter can be used to boost the protein level.

64. DIMMING DILL DIP

Preparation Time: 10 minutes

Total Time: 10 minutes

INGREDIENTS:

- 1 cup plain Greek yogurt
- 1/2 cup mayonnaise
- 2 tablespoons fresh dill, finely chopped
- 1 tablespoon lemon juice
- 1 clove garlic, minced
- Salt and black pepper to taste

For Garnish (Optional):

- Fresh dill sprigs
- Sliced cucumbers and carrots for dipping

INSTRUCTIONS:

1. Prepare the ingredients: mince the garlic and finely cut the fresh dill.
2. Combine Dip Base: Combine the plain Greek yogurt, lemon juice, minced garlic, mayonnaise, and chopped dill in a basin.
3. Add salt and black pepper to the dill dip according to your taste for a more subdued seasoning. Combine thoroughly.
4. Chill (Optional): Cover the dip and place it in the refrigerator for at least 30 minutes to allow the ingredients to mingle for better taste. Although optional, doing this step is advised.
5. Optional garnish:
6. Add some fresh dill sprigs to the fading dill dip before serving.
7. Serve: Arrange a selection of sliced carrots, cucumbers, or other vegetables for the dip.

NOTES:

- Adjust the salt, lemon juice, and garlic to suit your tastes.
- Use reduced-fat or light versions of mayonnaise and Greek yogurt for a lighter dip.

65. QUARTER PHASE QUINOA SALAD

Preparation Time: 15 minutes

Cooking Time: 15 minutes (for quinoa)

Total Time: 30 minutes

INGREDIENTS:

For the Salad:

- One cup of washed and cooked quinoa, following the directions on the package
- 1 cup cherry tomatoes,
- 1 cucumber cut in half,
- 1 diced
- bell pepper (any color),
- 1/2 diced
- red onion,
- 1/4 cups pitted and sliced
- Kalamata olives

For the Dressing:

- 3 tablespoons extra virgin olive oil
- 1 tablespoon red wine vinegar
- 1 teaspoon Dijon mustard
- 1 clove garlic, minced
- Salt and black pepper to taste
- chopped fresh herbs (parsley, basil, etc.)

INSTRUCTIONS:

1. For cooking, rinse quinoa cold. Mix one cup quinoa and two cups water or vegetable broth in a saucepan. After boiling, decrease heat to a simmer, cover, and let quinoa absorb water for 15 minutes. Cool, fork-fluff.
2. Mix cooked quinoa, cucumber, red onion, cherry tomatoes, and Kalamata olives in a big bowl. Crumble feta.
3. In a small bowl, blend extra virgin olive oil, red wine vinegar, Dijon mustard, minced garlic, salt, and black pepper for dressing. Spicy flavor.

4. Mix and Toss: Drizzle the quinoa and veggies with the dressing. Mix everything gently until thoroughly blended.
5. Chill (Optional): Before serving, cover and chill the Quarter Phase Quinoa Salad for at least 30 minutes to enhance the taste. Although optional, doing this step is advised.
6. Garnish and Serve: Before serving, sprinkle the salad with chopped parsley ba,sil, or other fresh herbs.

NOTES:
- Feel free to add other veggies, such as avocado, corn, or radishes, to customize the salad.
- Add some shrimp, chickpeas, or grilled chicken for extra protein.

66. RECEDING RADISH WRAPS

Preparation Time: 20 minutes

Total Time: 20 minutes

INGREDIENTS:

For the Filling:

- 1 cup cooked , shredded chicken or tofu
- 1/2 cup shredded carrots
- 1/2 cucumber, julienned
- 1/4 cup red bell pepper and thinly sliced
- 1/4 cup avocado, sliced
- 1/4 cup fresh cilantro leaves

For the Radish Wraps:

- 1 bunch of radishes, washed and trimmed
- Hummus or your favorite spread for assembling
- For Dipping Sauce (Optional):
- 2 tablespoons soy sauce
- 1 tablespoon rice vinegar
- 1 teaspoon sesame oil
- 1 teaspoon honey or maple syrup
- Sesame seeds for garnish

INSTRUCTIONS:

1. To prepare the filling, place the shredded chicken or tofu, julienned cucumber, avocado slices, sliced red bell pepper, and fresh cilantro leaves in a dish. Mixing the components well is necessary.
2. Slice the radishes thinly lengthwise with a sharp knife or mandoline slicer to make thin, flexible wrappers. Using a paper towel, pat the radish slices dry to absorb any remaining moisture.
3. To assemble the wraps, place a slight coating of hummus or your preferred spread down the middle of a radish slice.
4. Spoon some of the fillings onto the slice of radish.
5. Fold and Secure: Fold the radish's sides over the filling, then roll it up. If needed, use toothpicks to hold the wrap in place.

6. Repeat: Continue using the remaining radish slices and filling similarly.
7. To prepare the Dipping Sauce (Optional), combine the soy sauce, rice vinegar, sesame oil, honey, or maple syrup in a small dish. Add sesame seeds as a garnish.
8. Present: Present the Recessing Radish Wraps alongside the optional dipping sauce.

NOTES:
- To avoid damaging the radish slices, handle them gently.
- Try varying the fillings and spreads to add some diversity.

67. LUNAR LAVENDER LEMONADE

Preparation Time: 15 minutes

Cooling Time: 1-2 hours (for chilling)

Total Time: 1 hour 15 minutes

INGREDIENTS:

- 1 cup fresh lemon juice
- 1 cup granulated sugar
- 6 cups water
- 1-2 tablespoons dried lavender buds (culinary grade)
- Ice cubes
- Lemon slices and fresh lavender sprigs for garnish

INSTRUCTIONS:

1. In a saucepan, combine one cup water and granulated sugar to produce lavender simple syrup. Stir the sugar over medium heat until completelydissolved.
2. Add the dried lavender buds to the simple syrup. After bringing the mixture to a simmer, turn off the heat.
3. Let the lavender steep in the syrup for ten to fifteen minutes. After straining out the lavender buds, let the simple syrup infused with lavender cool.
4. Prepare the Lemon Juice: Squeeze the lemons to yield one cup of fresh lemon juice while the lavender syrup cools.
5. Mix Lemon Juice and Lavender Syrup: In a big pitcher, combine the fresh lemon juice and simple syrup with lavender extract.
6. Add Water: Fill the pitcher with six glasses of water and thoroughly whisk to mix.
7. Chill: Place the Lunar Lavender Lemonade in the refrigerator for at least one or two hours to enable the flavors to combine and the beverage to cool.
8. To serve, place ice cubes in glasses and top with lavender lemonade when ready to serve.
9. Garnish: Add a fresh lavender sprig and a slice of lemon to each glass.

NOTES:

- Taste and adjust the sugar amount to your desired sweetness level. Because of their taste character, dried lavender buds of the highest caliber are advised.

68. DISAPPEARING DATE BARS

Preparation Time: 20 minutes

Baking Time: 20-25 minutes

Cooling Time: 1-2 hours

Total Time: 2 hours (including cooling time)

INGREDIENTS:

For the Crust:

- 1 cup old-fashioned oats
- 1 cup all-purpose flour
- 1/2 cup brown sugar, packed
- 1/4 teaspoon baking soda
- 1/2 cup unsalted butter, melted
- 1/2 cup chopped nuts (walnuts or almonds), optional

For the Date Filling:

- 2 cups pitted dates, chopped
- 1 cup water
- 1 tablespoon lemon juice
- 1/2 teaspoon vanilla extract

INSTRUCTIONS:

1. Oven Prep: Set the oven's temperature to 350°F, or 175°C. Butter a 9 x 9-inch baking dish.
2. Prepare the Crust:
3. Oats, brown sugar, baking soda, and all-purpose flour should all be combined in a mixing dish.
4. After the butter has melted, add the ingredients and stir until thoroughly mixed.
5. Stir in the chopped nuts if using.
6. Press mixture evenly into prepared baking pan bottom.
7. Bake the Crust: Bake the crust for 10 to 12 minutes, or until it is just beginning to brown. Remove it from the oven and set it aside.
8. To prepare the date filling, combine chopped dates, water, and lemon juice in a saucepan.

9. Mixing occasionally over medium heat for 5–7 minutes thickens the sauce and softens the dates. Whisk in vanilla after removing from heat.
10. Rebake: Place the pan back in the oven and continue baking for ten to fifteen more minutes or until the date filling is set and the sides are brown.
11. Cool: After 10 minutes in the pan, transfer the disappearing date bars to a wire rack to continue cooling.
12. Cut and Serve: After the bars have cooled, cut them into rectangles or squares. Have fun!

NOTES:
- You may change the sweetness of the date filling by varying the amount of sugar added.
- For the crust, experiment with various nuts or combinations.

69. DIMINISHED DARK CHERRY CRISP

Preparation Time: 15 minutes

Baking Time: 35-40 minutes

Total Time: 55-60 minutes

INGREDIENTS:

For the Cherry Filling:

- 4 cups dark cherries, pitted and halved
- 1/2 cup granulated sugar
- 2 tablespoons cornstarch
- 1 tablespoon lemon juice
- 1/2 teaspoon almond extract (optional)

For the Crisp Topping:

- 1 cup old-fashioned oats
- 1/2 cup all-purpose flour
- 1/2 cup brown sugar, packed
- 1/4 teaspoon cinnamon
- 1/4 teaspoon salt
- 1/2 cup unsalted butter and cold and cubed

INSTRUCTIONS:

1. Preheat the Oven: Set the temperature to 190°C or 375°F. Coat a × 9-inch baking pan with oil.
2. Get the Cherry Filling ready.
3. Put the almond extract (if using), lemon juice, cornstarch, granulated sugar, and dark cherries in a bowl. Toss the cherries until they are uniformly covered.
4. Spread the reduced cherry mixture equally in the bottom of the baking dish that has been prepared.
5. To make the crispy topping, combine the oats, brown sugar, cinnamon, all-purpose flour, and salt in a separate bowl.
6. Curl the butter and add it to the mixture. Stir the butter into the dry ingredients with your hands or a pastry cutter until they resemble coarse crumbs.
7. Sprinkle Topping: Distribute crispy topping evenly over cherry mixture in baking dish.

8. Bake: Bake for 35–40 minutes in a preheated oven until the cherry filling bubbles and the topping is golden brown.
9. Let cool: Wait 15–20 minutes before serving the reduced dark cherry crisp.
10. Warm and serve with vanilla ice cream.

NOTES:

➢ Adjust the amount of sugar in the cherry filling dependingAdjust the amount of sugar in the cherry fillingbased on your particular liking and the sweetness of the cherries.
➢ Try chopping some nuts (walnuts or almonds) and adding them to the crisp topping for an added crunch.

70. WILTED WANING WATERCRESS SOUP

Preparation Time: 15 minutes

Cooking Time: 20 minutes

Total Time: 35 minutes

INGREDIENTS:

- 1 bunch of watercress, tough stems removed
- 1 tablespoon olive oil
- 1 onion, chopped
- 2 cloves garlic, minced
- 3 medium potatoes, peeled and diced
- 4 cups vegetable or chicken broth
- Salt and black pepper to taste
- 1 cup milk or cream (optional)
- Fresh lemon juice (optional for serving)

INSTRUCTIONS:

1. To prepare the watercress, give it a good wash, trim off any tough stems, and coarsely slice the sensitive stems and leaves.
2. Sauté the onion and garlic: Heat olive oil in a large pot on medium. Add minced garlic and onions. Sautéed onions should be translucent and fragrant.
3. Add the potatoes: Toss the diced potatoes in the onion-garlic mixture in the saucepan, coatingughly.
4. Add Broth: As you pour the vegetable or chicken broth in, make sure the potatoes are covered. After boiling, reduce heat and simmer until potatoes are tender.
5. Wilt Watercress: Add chopped watercress to the saucepan with the potatoes when they're tender. Let watercress wilt into the broth for a few minutes.
6. Blend Soup: Blend the soup in stages or with an immersion blender until smooth.
7. Before serving, season soup with salt and black pepper. If needed, add broth for consistency.
8. Optional: For a creamier texture, stir in 1 cup of milk or cream. Heat the soup without allowing it to boil after adding the dairy.
9. To serve, ladle the soup into bowls of wilted, waning watercress. If desired, pour a little fresh lemon juice over each dish.

NOTES:
- You may change the soup's thickness by adding or removing broth.
- Before serving, consider adding a squeeze of lemon juice to the entire pot if you like your food sour.

THE END

Printed in Great Britain
by Amazon